Facilitating a Collegial Department in Higher Education

Jossey-Bass Resources for Department Chairs

Books

Jeffrey L. Buller, *Academic Leadership Day by Day: Small Steps That Lead to Great Success*

Jeffrey L. Buller, *The Essential Department Chair: A Practical Guide to College Administration*

Don Chu, *The Department Chair Primer: Leading and Managing Academic Departments*

Robert E. Cipriano, *Facilitating a Collegial Department in Higher Education: Strategies for Success*

Christian K. Hansen, *Time Management for Department Chairs*

Mary Lou Higgerson, *Communication Skills for Department Chairs*

Mary Lou Higgerson and Teddi A. Joyce, *Effective Leadership Communication: A Guide for Department Chairs and Deans for Managing Difficult Situations and People*

Daryl Leaming, *Academic Leadership: A Practical Guide to Chairing the Department, Second Edition*

Daryl Leaming, *Managing People: A Guide for Department Chairs and Deans*

Jon Wergin, *Departments That Work: Building and Sustaining Cultures of Excellence in Academic Programs*

Dan Wheeler et al., *The Department Chair's Handbook, Second Edition*

Journal

The Department Chair

Online Resources

Visit www.departmentchairs.org for information on online seminars, articles, book excerpts, and other resources tailored especially for department chairs.

Facilitating a Collegial Department in Higher Education

Strategies for Success

Robert E. Cipriano

Foreword by Jeffrey L. Buller

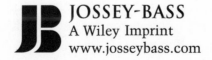

JOSSEY-BASS
A Wiley Imprint
www.josseybass.com

Published by Jossey-Bass
A Wiley Imprint
989 Market Street, San Francisco, CA 94103-1741—www.josseybass.com

Jossey-Bass books and products are available through most bookstores. To contact Jossey-Bass directly call our Customer Care Department within the U.S. at 800-956-7739, outside the U.S. at 317-572-3986, or fax 317-572-4002.

Jossey-Bass also publishes its books in a variety of electronic formats. Some content that appears in print may not be available in electronic books.

Library of Congress Cataloging-in-Publication Data

Cipriano, Robert E., date
  Facilitating a collegial department in higher education : strategies for success / Robert E. Cipriano ; foreword by Jeffrey L. Buller. – 1st ed.
      p. cm. — (Jossey-Bass resources for department chairs ; 130)
  Includes bibliographical references and index.
  ISBN 978-0-470-90301-8; 978-1-118-10763-8 (ebk); 978-1-118-10764-5 (ebk); 978-1-118-10769-0 (ebk)
  1. Universities and colleges—United States—Administration.   I. Title.
  LB2341.C546 2011
  378.73–dc22

                                                                2011014359

Printed in the United States of America
FIRST EDITION
HB Printing   10 9 8 7 6 5 4 3 2 1

Contents

To the Eight Women Wonders of the World:

To my precious daughters, Michele and Jennifer—
two of my dearest friends in life

To my two equally precious granddaughters, Amanda and Julia—
both bring immeasurable joy to me on a daily basis

To my loving wife and life's partner for forty-eight years, Raffaela—
she remains my dearest friend and loving companion

In loving memory of my grandmother, Theresa; my mother-in law,
Angie; and my mother, Rose—not a day goes by that I don't
remember their gift of love

Foreword

If you browse through the program of almost any conference devoted to administrative development today, you're likely to be amazed by the sheer number of sessions and presentations dealing with collegiality (or the lack thereof). Deans and department chairs are constantly challenged by the need to engender greater civility in their professional environments, no matter whether they're working at institutions large or small, public or private, newly created or blessed with a long tradition. We're all striving for good, open, and transparent communication as a means of achieving our goals in education and research and helping our programs succeed globally. Academic disciplines thrive when diverse perspectives can be shared without differences of opinion becoming the basis for rancorous personal attacks and when colleagues work together harmoniously without succumbing to group think. The big question, of course, is, How in the world can you do that?

In the chapters that follow, Bob Cipriano—one of the foremost voices in the area of administrative leadership today—provides a great deal of insight into where a lot of academic departments go wrong in their efforts to achieve civility, what works best, and how case law has affected the way in which collegiality is addressed in higher education today. There's not a page in this book that didn't teach me something important, and I'm coming away from it with a lot of great ideas for my own program that I can't wait to start trying. If you haven't yet had the privilege of experiencing Bob in person at a workshop or in a consultancy, that's a pity, but this book is the next best thing. You'll have a lot of opportunities to see his wit in operation, to benefit from his data-driven analyses of what works in academic leadership today, and to gain insights from his vast experience. If that's not enough, Bob's colleague Ellen Beatty has created a truly useful resource in Chapter Six, where she examines the issue of collegiality within the larger institutional environment, offering a wealth of practical advice about how chairs can partner with other administrators to improve the professional environment more broadly than is possible in the department alone.

If you're a regular reader of *The Department Chair*—and if you're not, then shame on you: you should be—you're already familiar with the surveys Bob conducts each year with Richard Riccardi. Those studies have been invaluable in giving administrators accurate information about how department chairs view their positions, what they regard as important, and what types of training they value most. You'll find the fruits of that work in this book as well, and it consistently demonstrates the importance that administrators place on good communication, making a positive difference in their disciplines, and creating an environment in which ideas can be explored *civilly and collegially*. But how those goals can be achieved and how they can best be incorporated into the structure of roles and rewards found throughout higher education today . . . *that* is a task that has so far eluded colleges and universities of all sizes and missions. In the pages that follow, Bob makes a major contribution toward filling this gap. Whether your interest is in discovering what case law has established about the proper role of collegiality at institutions of higher education, creating a practical plan for promoting collegiality in your own department, or developing a university-wide strategy for promoting positive and collegial discourse, *Facilitating a Collegial Department in Higher Education: Strategies for Success* has the answers you're looking for.

But what I think Bob's greatest contribution in this book is something that goes far beyond the topic of collegiality itself. By the time you reach Chapter Three you'll be discovering ways of not only avoiding something negative (*in*civility, *un*collegial behavior), but also of building something positive (enthusiastic, collaborative progress). The department chair who's a genuine academic leader is someone who's interested in creating an environment in which students learn best, faculty scholarship is innovative, and the entire campus community is fully engaged in the mission of higher education. This vision becomes possible as more and more chairs incorporate into their daily activities the ideas that are explored here. Its title, after all, is *Facilitating a Collegial Department in Higher Education: Strategies for Success*, not *Rescuing an Uncivil Department*. The goal is always to keep our eyes on the affirmative.

Now if we could only find some way of making Bob a bit more collegial himself . . .

June 2011   Jeffrey L. Buller
Dean, Harriet L. Wilkes Honors College
Florida Atlantic University
Jupiter, Florida

Facilitating a Collegial Department in Higher Education

Introduction

Incivility and lack of collegiality are on the rise in institutions of higher education. This phenomenon can range from disputes and tension at one and to violence at the other. There are many departments that suffer from noncollegial, uncivil, and nasty encounters between faculty members, faculty members and staff, and faculty members and students. Department chairs must deal with these types of encounters on a regular basis. If you are a department chair, you may feel that this is just the way it is, that you must struggle on your own to deal with a noncollegial and downright nasty faculty member or a department culture in which civility is compromised. Don't!

From my many years of presenting information on collegiality and conflict management to chairs and deans, I have found that 80 to 100 percent of them have horror stories to tell regarding the vitriolic antics of a faculty member so you are certainly not alone in the frustrating challenge of reigning in a person spewing venom. The bad news is that this may be happening to you and your department. The good news is that there are proved strategies to put a stop to this noncollegial and uncivil behavior.

This book will provide the chair—whether a new chair or an experienced chair, whether a chair at a public or private college or university, whether a chair at a two-year community college or a comprehensive or Research 1 university—with the tools to effectively lead a department and negotiate through the potholes presented by toxic individuals who appear to be hell-bent on destroying the department.

We all realize that one mean-spirited, toxic person can render a department dysfunctional. This book is written for department chairs by a person who has served as a department chair for twenty-eight years and will provide a proactive approach based on my work with fellow chairs and deans throughout the country to lead a civil department. It will provide a template for department chairpersons to have in order to facilitate a collegial and civil department. Academic deans and assistant or associate deans should find this book a valuable resource as well.

The book has seven chapters, each focusing on various aspects regarding collegiality. Using a question-and-answer format to share the considerable knowledge, expertise, and experience of the people who were interviewed, it includes many colleagues' comments to offer the readers a balanced approach to the varied issues raised by the topics inherent in collegiality. The book is designed to be engaging and interactive for the readers. Most chapters also have a case study for the reader to think about. This book has a dual focus: (1) strategies for department chairs to use to deal with toxic colleagues and (2) the importance of fostering a collegial climate within the department. The important interrelationship of these two foci is explored throughout the book.

Chapter One provides an overview of collegiality, its operational definition, and traces the history of incivility in higher education. It explores the importance of collegiality and the role of the department chair. Using hypothetical statements of faculty members, the chapter asks the reader to determine what constitutes collegial or noncollegial behavior. The chapter concludes with practical strategies the chair can use to facilitate a collegial department.

Chapter Two provides a tool kit that chairs can use to facilitate a collegial department through hiring a person with the potential to be a civil colleague. It includes questions pertaining to collegiality a search committee may ask a perspective new faculty member during an interview. A code of conduct, an academic honesty statement, and the bylaws to establish a council of academic chairs is included. It provides examples of pertinent forms for readers to use in their entirety or to adapt to their specific needs.

Chapter Three explores proved methods of what the department chair can do with a noncollegial faculty member. It emphasizes the point that the chair should not try to live with noncollegiality until her term of chair is over but to actively and proactively try to foster collegiality. Some tried and true leadership ideas are provided (celebrate people's successes, your values are more important than your techniques, and so on) that should enable a chair to grasp these concepts and readily apply them.

Chapter Four provides useful information concerning managing conflict within the department. Productive dissent is the goal, whereby ideas are discussed in an atmosphere of trust and respect. Destructive conflict is personal and can essentially reduce a department to rubble.

Chapter Five provides an overview of what the university can do to reign in a vitriolic faculty member. A department chair should not be left to deal alone with a noncollegial faculty member who is wreaking havoc on a department. The department chair can use the college or university's myriad resources to deal with an unruly, disrespectful faculty member. This chapter provides insight about the responsibilities of the college or university as a whole to put in place a systemic approach to civility that is central to the overall success of the campus.

Chapter Six is written by Ellen Beatty who has served successfully as a dean, an associate vice president, and a vice president for academic affairs. Beatty draws on her considerable expertise to specifically detail how the central administration (consisting of academic deans, vice presidents, provosts, human resources, student government, and so on) can develop the support system that a department chair needs. In this chapter, she explores strategies for how the chair can involve others in academic leadership positions when dealing with a problem faculty member. She also provides the reader with a very helpful discussion of the prevalence of, and the challenges associated with, cyberbullying within institutions of higher education

Chapter Seven presents case law regarding collegiality in higher education. An overview of what the courts have ruled is provided. It looks at tenure documents on the subject of collegiality from two universities and presents arguments for and against the use of collegiality as a criterion for tenure decisions. The role of the department chair as the connecting link between faculty members and administration is articulated. The importance of the chair-dean relationship cannot be overstated. When a noncollegial faculty member aims his or her profane fusillade at peers and students, it is imperative that the chair is supported by the dean.

The Appendix is a summary of a four-year national study that examines department chairs: who they are, what they do, what they are expected to do, and ultimately, what drives them to want to be in their current position.

The book can be read a chapter at a time as a resource book to draw on when a chair needs help with a particular challenge. A chair can also, when and if time permits, read the entire book in one sitting. Department chairs occupy a pivotal position in institutions of higher education. On a daily basis a chair is asked to perform myriad tasks, not the least of which is to intervene in a department kerfuffle caused by a piquant faculty member. The road to success is parlous indeed. However, it should not be the sole responsibility of a department chair to rein in a toxic faculty member. Unfortunately, it appears as if this has devolved into the chair's duty. To bring civility to a department and to a campus is a university-wide responsibility. To do otherwise will merely serve to discourage quality individuals from aspiring to the distinguished role of respect and admiration that should be accorded a department chair. It is my fervent wish that this book can help lighten the considerable load of my colleagues and peers who serve as department chairs.

1

COLLEGIALITY AND CIVILITY IN HIGHER EDUCATION

The words of the Evil Ones . . . The words of the
Unmentionable Times . . .

—Ayn Rand (1995)

A friend of mine, Mark, told me a story that is much more than
an urban legend. Mark is from Texas. Why this fact is important
will become crystal clear in roughly three minutes as you continue to read on. Mark was standing in line at the international
airport in Singapore waiting to board an airplane to return to
the United States. He was the sixth person in line. He heard, as
he is sure everyone in the country of Singapore heard as well, a
very large man screaming at a frail, young, and peaceful-looking
counter person representing the airline. The man was yelling,
"I'm from Texas" (I told you to be patient for the Texas connec-
tion). "In the U.S. of A. we do things the right way. If this was
America I could upgrade without a question. But, by your inability to communicate coherently, it's obvious you are not from
America." The young woman continued to smile and answered
the man's loud attack with kindness, gentleness, and a quiet demeanor. Finally the man stormed away. When Mark went to the
counter for his seat assignment he felt obligated to apologize for
two reasons: (1) he is American and (2) he is from Texas. He
said that he was sorry for how abusive and demeaning the man
was to her. She indicated it was quite all right. Mark stated how
impressed he was with her calm deportment. He asked her if
she had special training in dealing with difficult, loud, and

obnoxious people. She replied that, no, she did not have training in this area. Mark asked her how she was able to be so pleasant under this nasty onslaught. She softly replied: "As he was screaming at me I kept thinking: he is flying to Columbia, South Carolina, . . . but his luggage is flying to . . . Colombia, South America."

Although this aphorism is clearly not within the academic culture in which we work, the result of this man's belligerent and demeaning behavior did evoke a somewhat predictable response: uncivil and nasty behavior elicits like behavior and like responses aimed toward the person who precipitated the encounter. This account is not an indictment of people from Texas. If the traveler had been civil and respectful to this person who was doing her job to the best of her ability, both he and his luggage would have arrived at the same destination. Civility and collegiality can also be strong allies in facilitating a department to arrive at the same destination. Yet we seem to be in short supply of civility these days.

What happened to civility? screamed the front page of *USA Today* (della Cava, 2009). Della Cava cites the following illustrative examples of this scorching headline:

- Kanye West—Suggested to Taylor Swift that Beyoncé should have won MTV's Video Music Awards; stated in front of a live television audience of countless people.
- Serena Williams—Lost the U.S. Open semifinal match with an expletive-laced tirade whereby she threatened a woman judge with bodily harm; subsequently fined $82,500.
- South Carolina Republican Representative Joe Wilson screaming, "You lie!" at President Obama during the State of the Union address.
- And in August 2010 Steven Slater, a Jet Blue flight attendant, after an on-board confrontation with an uncivil passenger, cursed out the passenger on the airplane's

intercom and abruptly left the plane by sliding down the emergency chute. His actions evoked a visceral response from the public: he was cast as somewhat of a hero and became an overnight media icon. People throughout the country showed their support and understanding of his reaction to dealing with an uncivil and nasty person.

These stories are just an example of the incivility that seems to mark much of our interactions and relationships these days. Unfortunately, this is also true for the world of higher education.

Incivility in Higher Education

Many of us have seen how a toxic, uncivil, noncollegial faculty member can destroy a once-great department. Such a person can create an unhealthy and poisonous environment that deleteriously affects the entire department. Mean-spirited and uncivil people cause much damage to those they belittle, to the bystanders (students, staff, and department peers) who suffer the ripple effects, to the overall department performance, and to themselves. Faculty members who previously were stalwarts in the department simply disengage so that they are no longer targets to the malicious onslaught of nastiness perpetuated by this venomous person. A vicious cycle follows as faculty members retreat so they are not part and parcel to this person's nasty attacks, students change majors because the climate in the department is contaminated, the chair becomes frustrated in her attempt to stop this escalating asperity, and the administration is swept up in the detritus of this department. And in some cases, the president and provost declare fiscal emergency and the department is dissolved. This may seem an unlikely scenario but it has happened in the past in more or less the same sequence.

The academy does not have a glorious past in investing in a climate and culture of civility. Documented cases of abuse go back as far as Harvard in 1636 when the wealthy acted against the underprivileged and pitiable to prevent them from attending the university. Unfortunately, academe has not become a much more civil place to work in the intervening years.

Incivility is on the rise within institutions of higher education. This fact was unfortunately seen in the extreme in January 2010 when Amy Bishop brought a 9-millimeter handgun to a faculty meeting and allegedly shot six fellow faculty members, killing three. In another incident, Bruno Ullrich, associate professor at Bowling Green University, was suspended after making verbal threats to colleagues in February 2010. Although these are extreme cases, there are many noncollegial, uncivil, and nasty encounters that occur in the academy on a regular basis.

> "Academe, with its rigid hierarchy in what is supposed to be a collaborative culture, is a natural incubator for conflict."
>
> —P. Fogg (2003)

I have spoken with countless department chairs, deans, and provosts who recount horror stories of how one cruel and venomous person spewing nastiness and malice in a vindictive manner caused a department to be dissolved.

Changing Dynamics of Higher Education

The landscape of higher education for the sixteen hundred public and two thousand private institutions of higher education is rapidly changing and constantly evolving (ostensibly on a daily basis). Fueled by economic uncertainty, universities struggle with the perfect storm of increased student demand coupled with diminishing resources. Administrative edicts of doing "more with less" are falling on fewer ears as the academy ages into retirement and vacant positions remain unfilled.

In addition, there are other factors, both positive and negative, that challenge universities and faculty members and can lead to an increasingly uncivil workplace. Here are some of the factors adding to an uncivil workplace in institutions of higher education, which for ease of reading are placed in five distinct categories:

Students
- More diverse students
- Perception by faculty of less-qualified students
- Perception by faculty of less-motivated students

Faculty
- Professors' work subject to scrutiny and validation by their peers
- Academic freedom
- Shared governance
- Internal tension between faculty members who must choose between loyalty to profession or discipline and loyalty to their institution
- More rigorous promotion and tenure standards
- Ratcheting up of the workload
- More competition between departments for limited resources
- More competition among members of the same department to obtain resources
- Power imbalances—tenured versus nontenured faculty, full professor versus assistant professor, full-time faculty versus contingent faculty, and so on
- Changing face of the professoriate in terms of gender, age, and race
- The holy grail of higher education—AKA tenure
- Politics of specialization, which has hurt collaboration
- Overuse of, and overreliance on, e-mail as a mode of communication
- Eroding of faculty member benefits

- Job insecurity—job market shrinking
- Reward structures—rewards individual accomplishments rather than collaboration
- Shift to online education
- Unionization of faculty members and staff on the rise

Administration

- Hierarchical bureaucratic model that has led to miscommunication and distrust between faculty and administration
- Liberal arts curriculum versus vocationalism
- More top-down decisions, which do more harm than good
- Bureau-pathology—universities are underled and overmanaged
- High turnover rates of deans, vice presidents, provosts, and presidents

Budget and income

- More money and resources available in the 1970s and 1980s for research than at the present time
- Dwindling department budgets
- Decreased support for higher education by the states
- Institutional operating funds that flow to intercollegiate athletic programs rather than academics

Social climate

- Mission creep—straying from the core values of teaching and service in favor of the market share
- Turmoil of the 1960s led to a decrease of a culture of civility.
- Expectations to do (much) more with (much) less
- Heightened campus politics

- Corporate culture influence
- Affirmative action controversy
- New campus culture wars
- Competition of the for-profit sector in higher education

Many of these factors are new to faculty; they may not have had to address anything like it in their entire career. Thus, they may trigger emotional anxiety and insecurities and strain personal relationships. This is relevant to new faculty members as well because they have the additional stress of meeting promotional and tenure standards. Responding to these stressors may, in turn, be causative factors that elicit noncollegial behavior on the part of an individual toward students, staff, peers, and colleagues.

These challenges have taken place within a relatively brief time period. Most institutions of higher education are not prepared to move quickly and proactively to meet these challenges head on. Institutions of higher education move in a ponderous manner. Colleagues have told me that their institutions of higher education, although not exactly a dystopia, conduct the business of education in a slow, ponderous way primarily because of its many layers of bureaucracy. Higher education has been characterized by bureau-pathology—it is overmanaged and underled! This description is offered as a note of caution when strategies are presented regarding how institutions of higher education can implement policies to facilitate a more collegial campus.

Institutions of higher education go about the business of education with the efficiency of the Department of Motor Vehicles and the compassion of the Internal Revenue Service.

Gappa, Austin, and Trice (2007) wrote that "challenging times require everyone's efforts, the mutual commitment of all stakeholders to the well-being of their college or university. All members of the academic community must accept responsibility and work together to ensure high-quality, supportive academic workplaces where each member is respected and valued for his or her contributions" (p. 157).

We are truly at a crossroads in higher education and much of the systemic change falls on a position that continues to be ill-defined with incumbents who are ill-prepared to address myriad challenges they are facing daily: the department chair. Destined to be agents of that change by their central position in the organizational hierarchy, department chairs play a leadership role that few understand, yet all would agree is critical to the transformative revitalization of departments and to campuswide civility and collegiality.

The Importance of Civility in Higher Education

A campus culture that values collegiality and civility is among the most important contributions a university can make. Academic departments recognize the desirability of a collegial environment for faculty members, students, and professional employees and that such an environment should be maintained and strengthened throughout the university. In an environment enhanced by trust, respect, and transparency faculty members can be revivified so that they can play an active and responsible role in academic matters. A collegial relationship is most effective when peers work together to carry out their duties and responsibilities in a professional manner.

Universities are one of the last bastions where people can share divergent ideas and thoughts. In fact, both shared governance and academic freedom are endemic to sharing knowledge—with students as well as with colleagues and peers. Collegiality does not impinge on the freedom of faculty members to make their views known.

Collegial or Noncollegial, You Make the Call

1. Dr. Thunder yells at faculty members and students.

2. Dr. Will Doitt is a pleasant person and a good teacher.

3. Dr. Nix Doitt refuses to advise students and does not serve on any department or university committees.

4. Dr. Tempest, the former chair of the department, declines to attend department meetings.

5. Dr. Fairly volunteers to serve on university-wide and department committees.

6. Dr. Carp chronically complains . . . about everything and everyone.

7. Dr. Chitchat spends hours gossiping.

8. Dr. Humility facilitates the functioning of all collaborating assignments in the department.

9. Dr. Contrary does not, and steadfastly refuses to, collaborate with colleagues.

10. Dr. Unbendable has developed a reputation for being inflexible.

11. Dr. Numb is insensitive to feelings of colleagues when commenting on their teaching, scholarship, or service.

12. Dr. Delightful always agrees to disagree without being disagreeable.

13. Dr. Catalyst offers emotional support to colleagues who are experiencing a personal tragedy.

14. Dr. Gracious responds promptly and politely to e-mail and phone voice messages from colleagues and students.

15. Dr. Forbearance is tolerant of opposing opinions of colleagues.

16. Dr. Browbeat is a bully to the nontenured colleagues in the department.

(*continued*)

(*continued*)

Perhaps the person reading this book has made a determination that she would be elated to have faculty represented by numbers 2, 5, 8, 12, 13, 14, and 15 as colleagues. Conversely, she may have decided that faculty represented by numbers 1, 3, 4, 6, 7, 9, 10, 11, and 16 are people to avoid at all costs. At first blush, the majority of people will have made the same determination. A more thorough synthesis and analysis, however, is required so that one can see beyond a one-sentence description to what may lie beneath. Therefore, what is taken as 100-percent factual may in reality constitute a verisimilitude. Therein lies a monumental dilemma that requires a great deal of cogitation to resolve. For example, perhaps Dr. Fairly (number 5, "volunteers to serve on university-wide and department committees") refuses to keep office hours, misses his assigned classes, does not engage in scholarship, refuses to advise students, is a terrible teacher, and so on. And Dr. Thunder (number 1, "yells at faculty members and students") may be a great teacher, who tirelessly advises students, is an eminent scholar, a very successful grant getter, and so on. To accurately ascertain the collegiality of a colleague, coming to uniformity and agreement—throughout the university as a whole—of what constitutes collegial as well as noncollegial behavior is a vital step in fostering a civil, collegial university. This will also address the legitimate concerns of faculty members who believe that collegiality can be used as a code word for "getting" someone they do not get along with. One example of this is when a powerful senior faculty member's strong views on a subject may lead to "group think" for fear of reprisals against those who do not agree with him. Another example is when a nontenured person disagrees with a senior faculty member who will be evaluating the person for promotion and tenure decision. It is self-evident that faculty, administrators, and staff need to be educated about the ramifications of uncivil and noncollegial behavior. This edification should focus on its context, its contents, and its consequences to the department and the university as a whole.

Collegiality Operationally Defined

There has been much deliberation and outright confusion concerning the term *collegiality*. The following represents acceptable definitions of the word:

- As a noun *collegiality* means cooperative interaction among colleagues.
- As an adjective *collegial* means collective responsibility shared by each member of a group of colleagues with minimal supervision from above.
- To the many detractors *collegiality* is a code word for a person who is overweight, smokes, dresses badly, has a different way of seeing things, and so on.
- *Collegial* behavior does not imply mindless conformity or absence of dissent. Rather, operationalizing collegiality as either a noun or an adjective enhances productive dissent, a basic tenet of the academy.

Gappa, Austin, and Trice (2007) wrote about the importance of collegiality and the fact that many people in the academy regularly refer to each other as colleagues. They wrote that "collegiality refers to opportunities for faculty members to feel that they belong to a mutually respected community of scholars who value each faculty member's contributions to the institution and feel concern for their colleagues' well-being" (p. 305).

Yet this sense of belonging can be torn apart by a hostile, nasty person discharging venomous rancor on a continuous and unswerving basis.

What we strive for in the academy is a healthy and respectful sharing of ideas and concepts where people feel free to express their divergent and oftentimes conflicting views. In fact, many historians consider this concept to be one of the hallmarks of higher education. We most certainly do not want affable Babbitts mimicking everything that a senior faculty member subscribes to or thinks. What we do want is dissent—more specifically, positive dissent. One of the dominant characteristics of higher education is that professors have opportunities to express their ideas openly and unafraid of castigation in the form of petty reprisals of a personal nature. Discussions may be passionate. Discussions may become heated. But discussions should never become mean, nasty, or vindictive. Professionals may disagree, express their thoughts ardently, but never vindictively or personally.

Facilitating a culture of collegiality can be the synergetic agent of good relationships among members of a department—which all too often is severely missing. The clarion call can be agree to disagree without being disagreeable! It is clear that constructive arguments over ideas—but not personal arguments over ideas—drive greater performance and creativity. It is important for the chair as well as other faculty members in the department to deal with and, as stridently and quickly as necessary, address the malefactors on the staff. Contagion from uncivil and venomous faculty members can create significant short-term and long-term threats to the department. They become a ubiquitous presence that stifles the culture and productivity in a department. However, when people engage in disagreements over ideas in an atmosphere of mutual trust and respect, they develop stronger ideas and perform better. The end product is often superior to one person working alone in isolation. Working on a solution to a problem in an environment built on trust, reverence, and civility can awaken people from their self-afflicted torpor and enable them to contribute a meaningful resolution to a quandary.

Several studies have documented the importance of maintaining civility in a department:

- Departments that function most effectively have demonstrated an ability to work collegially; they view themselves as a collective whole, a team (Pew Higher Education Roundtable, 1996).

- Climate, collegiality, and culture are more important to early career faculty than workload, money, and tenure clarity (Collaborative on Academic Careers in Higher Education, 2007).

- Misunderstood, disrespected, and disenfranchised faculty and administrators exit universities, most often citing conflict and miscommunication as the primary reasons (Kezar, 2000).

- Lack of civility in a department leads to faculty disengagement. Once productive faculty members who experience a negative, often traumatic, incident in the department or university simply extricate themselves from collegial discussions, campus and university service, department socials, and faculty mentoring (Cipriano, 2009b).

- In a study of department chairs at community colleges in Connecticut, the chairs reported their biggest challenge was a lack of collegiality (Cipriano, 2009a).

The Challenging and Complex Role of the Department Chair

I have been privileged to have been invited to many campuses to speak with department chairs and academic deans regarding the chair's role in facilitating a collegial department. When questioning the chairs and deans in attendance at the various campuses, fully 80 to 100 percent indicated that they had at least one noncollegial or uncivil faculty member in their department. I have spoken with countless chairs, deans and provosts who recount horror stories of how one venomous person spewing nastiness and malice in a vindictive manner caused a department to be dissolved. In one university on the East Coast, a department was dissolved and the dean and provost blamed the chair who couldn't "handle" the problem of two tenured faculty members who constantly spewed venom. Yet the dean and provost had totally abrogated their professional responsibilities to intervene on behalf of the students, professional staff, faculty members, and department chair.

The department chair is often placed in the untenable position of resolving conflicts between and among faculty members in their department. After all, the thinking goes, the chair is the front line in settling disputes. However, few department chairs have been adequately trained to know with any degree of exactitude and confidence how to dispel a problem before it degenerates into a long-standing feud that can render a department dysfunctional. Lucas and Associates (2000) wrote that "a leader is needed, one who can manage resistance and conflict so that the department is strengthened and faculty are revitalized rather than demoralized by the process. A courageous department chair who is knowledgeable about the steps to take and what to expect at each stage is the ideal person to launch such a change, which can transform a department" (p. 14).

The Lynchpin of a University

I have always viewed the department chair as a service position and the lynchpin of a university. Although chairs have always occupied a pivotal role in higher education, the position is often poorly defined, and deans, faculty members, students, and chairs themselves may have conflicted expectations about the functions of the role. The "job description" of a department chair is ill-defined and ambiguous. In fact, most universities do not have a job description specifically for chairs. At best, many universities compile a laundry list of job duties and responsibilities that chairs are expected to perform. Suffice it to say that the chair's role is changing. In fact the chair's role has morphed into a large and varied multiplicity set of skills, not the least of which is managing and leading a civil, respectful, and collegial department. The road to a successful reign of chairing a department is highly reliant, if not totally dependent, on having the internal constituencies perform in a civil manner that optimally advances the mission of the department.

In addition, chairs function in a hybrid person-in-the-middle role. Chairs are not faculty members, per se. Most chairs do, however, consider themselves first and foremost faculty members rather than administrators. They are also not administrators in the true sense of the word. Their unique role is to serve as a liaison to bridge the gap between faculty and the administration. The role of a department chair has become more complex and, at the same time, more ambiguous.

It is true that the chair inhabits a vitally important role in the academy. It is also instructive to note that 75 percent of the chairs I have surveyed indicate they will go back on faculty when their term as chair ends. Department chairs are typically tenured faculty members who are appointed or elected into a position with no formal training in how to succeed in this managerial and leadership position.

The Power of the Chair

Department chairs set the tone and culture in their department.

A chair is short on both formal authority (granted from a higher level in the college or university) and positional authority (merely having a title). Chairs do, however, have personal

"A house divided against itself cannot stand."

—Abraham Lincoln, speech, Springfield, Illinois, June 16, 1858

"The beatings will continue until morale improves!"

—bumper sticker

power that is achieved by the respect and confidence that faculty members place in them. The chair wears many hats, given the particular circumstances he is faced with. The one-size-fits-all chair position does not exist with any degree of regularity. A multitude of skills are needed on a habitual and consistent basis. In my twenty-eight years of serving as department chair, I have always (okay, the last four years anyway) understood that I had very limited carrots or sticks to persuade faculty members to support my advocacy in moving the department in a specific (usually new) direction. My persuasive powers were called into play on a regular, almost-daily basis. I have had good working relationships with strong and supportive academic deans as well as pusillanimous deans. My positive relationships with the deans and vice presidents I have served under have made my life as department chair much easier. A dean or vice president can make a decision and very seldom, if ever, meet face-to-face with the people directly affected by that decision. Conversely, the chair works with and interacts with people on a regular, everyday basis. This permits greater scrutiny, questioning, and opportunities for noncollegiality to permeate within the department. Faculty members will in all likelihood support a chair who is perceived as being competent, honest, and fair, has good interpersonal and communicative skills, is widely respected (throughout campus and in her professional field), has well-earned credibility, is universally known to be trustworthy, and treats all people with respect and dignity. When the chair's behavior leads faculty members and staff to distrust him, and he is not thought to be trustworthy, problems ensue: small problems become large ones and large problems become monumental and cause detritus that influences and infiltrates the entire department.

There are myriad challenges confronting higher education, not the least of which is the fact that 40 percent of the 595,000 full-time faculty members are fifty-five years of age or older. In addition, tenure (a reward for excellent service and possibly the major reward for displaying a high degree of collegiality) is being attacked from within and outside of institutions of higher education. The chair can serve for as little as three years or as long as a lifetime. The average chair, however, serves for six years. Twenty percent of chairs leave the position each year. A further variable that bears mentioning is the fact that more than 96 percent of chairs have not been trained to serve as chair and the position's varied roles have not been thoroughly explained to them (Cipriano and Riccardi, 2010b). Given the fact that the chair is called on to demonstrate a vast array of technical and personal skills, the jury is still out concerning what makes the most effective chairs. An enormously successful grant getter, a master teacher, or a great scholar does not necessarily have the requisite skill set to chair a department.

What Draws Someone to Chair a Department? To Make a Difference

Given that a chair's work is difficult and challenging and the chair is often not given adequate training—why would someone take on this role? Since 2007, a colleague and I have been surveying department chairs throughout the country to help define who they are, what they do, what they are expected to do, and ultimately, what drives them to want to be in their current position. In 2007, we surveyed a state university system on the past, present, and future aspirations of department chairs (Cipriano and Riccardi, 2008) and found that department chairs set their own expectations at almost unrealistic levels: a "master of all trades." In 2008, we broadened the survey in scope and distance (Cipriano and Riccardi, 2010a), surveying chairs from across the country about their satisfaction level and reasons why they stay as department chairs. In this study, we were puzzled to find that more than 85 percent were either satisfied or very satisfied serving as chair, yet the number-one reason they remain in their position is that "no one else will do it." Further qualitative research resulted in modifications to the 2008 survey instrument as focus groups with chairs brought to light that "making a difference" was a key factor in becoming a department chair. It is important to note that many of the skills listed (such as leadership and problem solving) are simply not innate but can be taught in some type of instructional setting such as a chair's institute, where new chairs could be paired with internal mentors or, as Olwell (2009) suggests, individuals from outside the university ("coaches"). It is significant to repeat that more than 96 percent of those department chairs surveyed have never been trained or educated to serve in the critical role of department chair and almost 80 percent have never had formal management training.

However, it was directly through my personal discussions with current and former department chairs that something insightful came to light: this job was more than merely "money," more than just "career aspirations," and more than just a burden that no one else would shoulder. Like the master potter, chairs truly believed that they could mold their department into something meaningful, casting profound influence on faculty members and students, and ultimately shaping the legacy of their department.

A salient question that these data raise is, Given the empty tool set that many universities give to department chairs, how will they be able to, as Lucas and Associates (2000) write, "transform the department"? It is perhaps the adjective Lucas uses to describe department chairs—*courageous*—that provides us some insight into the qualities chairs must have in order to be successful. Such a quality is necessary to travel a road that is difficult at best, bridging the ever-widening gap between faculty and administration, and in these stress-filled times, many chairs are looking to just survive, not necessarily thrive. University administration must also do its part; in this period of academic and financial challenges, department chairs must be empowered with the means to make the difference they long to make. To paraphrase Gandhi, department chairs must be the change they wish to see in their department.

The Power of Collegiality

People who are true colleagues are explicitly united in a common purpose and respectful of each other's abilities to work toward that purpose. Therefore, the word *collegiality* can connote respect for another's commitment to the common purpose, goals, and strategic plan of the department and an ability to work toward it in a nonbelligerent manner. Generally, a peer who is collegial collaborates with others, fosters teamwork, resolves conflict, proactively assists and actively involves others, builds bridges among colleagues, promotes rapport, shows patience and respect when working with colleagues, and makes decisions about the department's operational efficiency based on a professional assessment, not a personal judgment. The importance of collegiality cannot be overstated in view of the fact that departments' work depends heavily on consensus.

I have been on campuses where the morale can only be described as parlous. Administrators were jabbing chairs from the left and faculty members were jabbing from the right until most chairs resembled St. Sebastian (the human pincushion). However, in spite of the morose environment on campus, some departments were upbeat, engaging, and enthusiastically looking forward to coming to work! It is undeniable that department chairs play a significant role in how productive and collegial their department is. Don Chu (2006) wrote that "for the academy to function best, there should be an atmosphere of trust, respect, and collegiality. Ideas are the coin of the realm in the academy, and ideas are most freely exchanged when faculty and staff value each other and respect each other's opinions. In the best departments, the climate is one that invites expression, exploration, and inquiry. If there is one area that chairs most directly impact, it is their department's climate" (p. 30). It is worth reiterating that a chair who is characterized as trustworthy, an excellent communicator, is highly visible (he walks the halls rather than relies on e-mails to "speak" with faculty members, staff, and students), and is available, is transparent and consistent and fair in working with faculty, staff, and students is on his way to becoming an excellent leader as a chair.

Question: "If you were hiring a chair, please rank in order of priority the importance of each factor: demonstrated expertise in (1) teaching, (2) scholarship, (3) collegiality, (4) service."

*   *   *

Answer: "(1) collegiality, (2) teaching, (3) scholarship, (4) service. Collegiality is critical for a chair. From my perspective, I want a chair who is collegial but also a strong leader—both on campus and in the discipline." —William F. Williams, provost and vice president for academic affairs, Slippery Rock University

Answer: "(1) collegiality/civility, (2) teaching, (3) scholarship, (4) service." —Roger L. Coles, interim dean, Graduate Studies, Central Michigan University

Answer: "(1) collegiality and leadership, (2) teaching, (3) service, (4) research—and if not active then teach more." —Walter H. Gmelch, dean, School of Education, University of San Francisco

Answer: "I would rank the factors in priority order: 1. teaching, 2. collegiality, 3. scholarship, and 4. service. I think many search committees informally apply this concept—this is based on comments such as, I don't know that I could work with this person or I would like to collaborate with this applicant, and so on." —Bruce W. Russell, dean, College of Business, Information, and Social Sciences, Slippery Rock University

Question: "In your role as dean, how important do you think it is to hire a department chair with a demonstrated behavior of being collegial and civil?"

* * *

Answer: "One of the most important roles of the department chair is to manage the culture of the department so that it is a civil and productive unit. As we know many times this task is like herding cats as faculty are independent thinkers and doers but the chair must bring faculty together as a collective—a team if possible!" —Walter H. Gmelch, dean, School of Education, University of San Francisco

How Chairs Can Facilitate a Positive Environment in Their Department

According to Chu (2006) department chairs can develop and maintain a productive atmosphere in their department by recognizing and implementing the following:

• Department climate is the chair's responsibility. Chairs are called on to represent the department, assign teaching schedules, evaluate faculty members, and control the budget. Therefore, the chair can make the department conducive to a productive entity or a place where no one wants to spend time.

- Chairs can have a positive effect on the department environment by modeling the characteristics they wish their faculty members, staff, and students to exhibit. Chairs are symbolic leaders. They must treat everyone with respect and dignity if they expect the same from their colleagues. Do not fall into the "do as I say not as I do" syndrome.

- The chair position is a service position. Chairs serve the faculty so that faculty in turn can serve their students. The most important ingredient of an institution of higher education is the intellectual capital of its faculty. Therefore, faculty members must be supported, especially by the department chair who works closely with faculty members on a daily basis.

- Chairs need to be knowledgeable and competent. Chairs who are unable to perform the countless tasks associated with the position quickly poison the atmosphere in the department. Chairs are required to perform many tasks that have fixed deadlines.

- The chair's work should be as transparent as possible. Information in the department, with the exception of privileged personnel matters, should be regularly shared. Budget, teaching schedule, advisee lists, short-term and long-range planning, mission statements, and so on should be translucent. Secrecy directly spoils the morale in a department.

- Chairs should see themselves as equal. Chairs need to see and deport themselves as no better or worse than other faculty members. Note that the chair serves an average of six years. He will most likely return to faculty when his turn as chair expires. Also, great ideas are not limited to one person. Chairs who consistently convey that they are equal to faculty will gain the trust and respect of their colleagues.

- Chairs must be objective. We all have our personal biases. The chair must not allow her personal interpretations to take over the department. The chair should listen to all sides, whether or not they are in concert with her beliefs, weigh the advantages and disadvantages of each side, and publicly convey the reasons the decision was made.

- Chairs must be credible. When a chair does what he says he will do, he is thought to be credible. Faculty members support the chair because he can be trusted to follow through on his promises.

- Chairs must respect all members of the department. Free department discourse can take place only in an environment built on trust and respect. The chair does set the tone. She must model respect for all individuals, both junior and senior faculty members, those who have a point of view similar to hers and those who do not, the staff, students, student workers, and so on.

- Chairs must be humble. Chairs who take credit for every success in the department destroy the climate in the department. Humility should be practiced with exactitude!

- Department climate is bolstered by demonstrations of appreciation for jobs well done. Public recognition should be part and parcel of a good department. Successes should be celebrated through announcements at meetings, published in department newsletters, e-mails, and in letters congratulating the accomplishment. A word of caution: do not overdue this and make a public disclosure for trivial things: "It's great that Dr. Thompson met her class two times in a row."

- Chairs need to protect the confidentiality of the privileged information they receive. People's private information must be treated with the greatest respect. A chair can lose his credibility and trustworthiness if confidential information is shared with other people.

CASE STUDY

Problem

You are the chair of a department consisting of thirteen full-time faculty members. Dr. Latest is a new tenure-track assistant professor in your department. He began working in your department during the fall semester. He is a very fine and popular teacher; students acknowledge that he cares about them and he is very well prepared and engaging in his classes. You know that he devotes a great deal of time preparing to teach his classes. Dr. Latest has a postdoctorate in research and measurements from a highly acclaimed university.

Dr. Ancient is a tenured full professor who has been in the department for thirty-seven years. He currently teaches a graduate research class, the same class he has taught for the past twenty-four years. The course is scheduled to be taught in the spring semester. His teaching evaluations from students are terrible. He is very defensive when you show him the student evaluations. His response is, "These students are not prepared for graduate school. They are lazy, unmotivated, and do not want to learn." You and other members in the department want Dr. Latest to teach this very important core required class. You realize that Dr. Latest will do a far superior job than Dr. Ancient in teaching this graduate course in research. However, you are fearful that if you make this decision Dr. Ancient will become uncivil, wreak havoc in the department, and make everyone's life miserable. More pointedly, you recognize that Dr. Latest's tenure decision could be compromised: Dr. Ancient chairs the department evaluation committee. He is also very friendly with a number of people serving on the university-wide tenure and promotion committee. What will you do?

- Tell Dr. Ancient that Dr. Latest will be teaching the course next semester.

- Have Dr. Ancient and Dr. Latest work it out between the two of them.
- Get the dean to make the decision.
- Tell Dr. Latest that Dr. Ancient has outlived his usefulness to the department, he is a bad teacher, but "it's his course to teach."
- Hold a department meeting whereby all the faculty advocate for Dr. Latest to teach the course.

Possible Solution

You do not want to do anything to publicly embarrass Dr. Ancient. Meet individually with him and indicate how important his legacy is at the university and in the department. As he is the senior faculty member in the department, ask him to serve as a mentor to Dr. Latest, helping him to teach effectively, conduct research, make presentations at conferences, and publish his research. Recommend that Dr. Latest co-teach the graduate research course with him next semester.

Resources

The following sources address the department chair's roles and responsibilities:

- *The Essential Department Chair* (Buller, 2006, pp. 50–55). Chapter Eight, "Promoting Collegiality," presents a cursory overview of the importance of collegiality. A department code of conflict is also provided.
- *The Department Chair Primer: Leading and Managing Academic Departments* (Chu, 2006, pp. 29–33). Chapter Five, "Department Climate," describes the chair's responsibilities in promoting a positive environment in his or her department.

- "What Is Unique About Chairs? A Continuing Exploration" (Cipriano and Riccardi, 2010c). This article reports the results of a three-year study of the responses of 727 department chairs across the country. The reader will find demographic information concerning chairs (gender, highest degree held, academic rank, and so on), personal information (degree of satisfaction in serving as chair, plans after term as chair ends, and so on), perception of the skills and competencies needed to function effectively as chair, and the tasks chairs need to perform that are deemed pleasant or unpleasant.

- *Work and Peace in Academe* (Coffman, 2005). This book assesses the nature of conflict within institutions of higher education and describes practical ways to resolve nonproductive disputes. Best practices in conflict management are presented.

- *Rethinking Faculty Work: Higher Education's Strategic Imperative* (Gappa, Austin, and Trice, 2007). This book articulates the profound challenges that higher education is facing. Chapter Five discusses collegiality and provides strategies that foster collegiality.

- *The Department Chair as Academic Leader* (Hecht, Higgerson, Gmelch, and Tucker, 1999). Although this book was written in 1999, it is still relevant today. The authors identify roles and responsibilities of department chairs as well as important functional topics. The book is organized into four parts: (1) roles and responsibilities, (2) the department and its people, (3) the department and its operations, and (4) the department and the university. All parts of the text refer to the department chair.

- *Faculty Incivility* (Twale and De Luca, 2008). This book provides a perspective on incivility and bullying in institutions of higher education. The history of incivility in higher education is explored, along with the major causes of incivility. The third and final part of the text offers strategic suggestions for dealing with incivility, aggression, bullying, and mobbing in the academic workplace.

Conclusion

Our society seems to be in short supply of civility these days. Sadly, this is also true for the world of higher education. A campus culture that values collegiality and civility is among the most important contributions a university can make. A collegial relationship is most effective when peers work together to carry out their duties and responsibilities in a professional and respectful manner. A vital first step in fostering a civil, collegial university is to determine objectively what constitutes collegial as well as noncollegial behavior. The chair is often called on to resolve a conflict in her department. Constructive arguments over ideas—but not personal arguments—drive greater performance and creativity. Faculty members will support a chair who is perceived as being competent, honest, and fair; has good interpersonal and communication skills; is respected; has credibility; is trustworthy; and treats all people with respect and dignity.

Chapter Two provides the reader with useful documents that can be used to enhance collegiality in the department. Included are seven questions designed to measure collegiality that search committees can ask a prospective faculty member during a job interview.

2

RESPECTFUL CODES AND HIRING FOR COLLEGIALITY

Once there was a man who carved a duck from a
block of wood. Asked how he did it, the man said,
"I just got rid of everything that didn't look like
a duck."

—*Bumper sticker*

I often wished I could get rid of everyone that was a malefactor and behaved in a disrespectful, uncivil, and noncollegial way. I have served for the better part of twenty-eight years as a chair of a department consisting of five full-time faculty members. During this time, four presidents, five provosts, six deans, and all original five faculty members have come and gone—either through retirements or leaving for another position in the academy. I have been able to withstand the bad times (for example, budget cuts inflicted by the state), the good times (for example, the state had a surplus in their budget), and the *really bad* times (for example, dealing with a very toxic, tenured faculty member in the department prior to my arrival on campus to serve as chair). I came to the position, as the great majority of chairs do, without any specific education or training in its myriad roles and responsibilities. I did receive keys to my office and an "atta-boy" from the dean. The good news was that my office had a window; the bad news was that it looked out onto a garbage-strewn parking lot!

The purpose of this chapter is to provide the readers with practical knowledge and information that can be used in a chair's daily work. The emphasis will focus on collegiality issues within the department. Useful documents are provided that chairs can rapidly use or adapt to their specific, unique situation. At the least, the materials provide examples of thoughtful and meaningful dialogue that chairs can initiate with their faculty colleagues to address collegiality issues that, in turn, could enhance the department culture.

Attributes Faculty Members Should Possess

I have conducted nine national studies of department chairs. The surveys asked the respondents to rate the most important factors for faculty members to possess to be awarded tenure, promotion in rank, merit pay, and reappointment. Chairs consistently rated the following factors in order of significance in faculty personnel decisions in their department:

- Teaching
- Research
- Publications
- Collegiality

The first three factors are certainly no surprise, but the fourth—collegiality—presents myriad challenges to faculty, administrators, and chairs.

Hiring for Collegiality

Two of the most important decisions a department and university can make are whom to hire and whom to tenure. Depending on the pool of candidates, departments may interview as many as three or four of the top contenders. The department must establish a search committee, determine relevant questions to ask the aspirants, and agree to a schedule. The following are topics that interviewers *may* bring up with candidates:

- Job-related questions
- Further review or clarification of information
- Why the applicant is seeking employment
- The kind of references an applicant would receive from former employers
- Why the applicant left his or her former employment
- Questions about specific prior training or work experience directly related to the performance requirements of the position
- What the applicant liked and disliked about his or her prior jobs
- The job duties the applicant is interested in
- What hours and days an applicant is available or unavailable to work
- Allow the applicant to discuss what he or she feels is relevant to the position

The following are questions an interviewer must *not* ask:

- An applicant's race, color, religion, sex, national origin, or age
- Disabilities unless they prevent the candidate from performing the duties of the position
- Not job related
- The applicant's date or place of birth
- The applicant's maiden name, marital status, or children
- Where a spouse or parent works or resides
- If the applicant owns his or her place of residence

- The name of the applicant's bank or the amount of loans outstanding
- If the applicant has had his or her wages garnished or has declared bankruptcy
- Whether the applicant has served in the armed forces of another country
- What foreign language(s) he or she can speak, read, or write (unless job related)

How to Recognize and Support Collegiality

Although department chairs acknowledge that collegiality is a factor of great consequence, little research exists to suggest precision in the process of identifying how and under what circumstances this factor can be translated into the important decision of whom to hire.

Clearly there is a need to address ways to bring clarity and focus to this issue if department chairs and others with important insights about the hiring of personnel are to reap the rewards of difficult decisions generated in the process of recruiting and selecting university faculty. Chairs must lead the way in this regard. In conversations with colleagues, I have observed that collegiality is becoming a significant issue in departments and universities as a whole. At national conferences, those sessions exploring issues of collegiality and conflict management are the most well attended.

"I was a department chair for twenty-two of the thirty years I served in academe. And the longer I served, the clearer it became to me that my personal most-important hiring criterion for any new colleague was this: is this the kind of person I would like to spend time with for the rest of my career?"
—Timothy L. Hatfield, conversation, professor emeritus, counselor education, Winona State University

Collegiality Interview Questions

How can search committee members involved in the hiring process gain insight about a candidate's perceptions on the value of a "don't-worry-be-happy–why-can't-we-all-just-get-along" frame of mind? It is obvious that each candidate cannot be given a psychometric assessment such as the Minnesota Multiphasic Personality Inventory or the California Personality Inventory. To address this issue, in collaboration with five colleagues from Southern Connecticut State University, I developed and field-tested seven questions search committee members could ask when interviewing a candidate for a full-time faculty appointment. The intent of the questions is to help determine the collegiality of a potential faculty member. These questions have provided insight in assessing a candidate's views and values regarding collegiality and have helped determine how collegial a person was, is, and can be. These questions also allow the search committee to obtain the most significant responses within the area of collegiality and permit chairs to gain insight into a candidate's collegiality during an interview for a full-time faculty position within their department. These questions can be used in combination with other interview questions a search committee may ask.

1. What were your most creative contributions to promoting rapport among your colleagues?
2. Every department has its own "dysfunctionality quotient." In your last position, what were the quirks and how did you deal with them?
3. In what areas do you typically have the least amount of patience in working with your fellow faculty members?
4. If we were to ask your colleagues to describe your strengths and weaknesses in communicating with other faculty members, students, and management, what would they say?

5. Tell us about a conflict you had with a colleague in the past that, looking back, you would have handled differently.

6. All of us have core principles, values, or beliefs that we view as nonnegotiable. What issues would cause you to "go to the mat"?

7. Which of the following three factors would play the most significant role in your decision to accept the offer from this institution: (a) the university, (b) the position you are applying for, or (c) the people you would be working with?

Question 1: What Were Your Most Creative Contributions to Promoting Rapport Among Your Colleagues?

This question assumes that the candidate's last faculty appointment was beset with a lack of respect and collegiality among peers. Most faculty members typically identify their achievements via their ability to teach in a classroom, conduct and publish research, pursue scholarly activities, and provide service to the department, university, and community (as opposed to getting along with peers). This question is critical if your goal is to identify if the candidate came from a noncollegial department and the relative importance she places on getting along in a collegial department. Regardless of whether (or to what degree) your department espouses the ability to get along, finding people who look beyond their immediate functional areas to reduce conflict will have a direct impact on the climate within the department.

Creativity in this case has nothing to do with "artsy" stuff, research publications, or candidates' need for aesthetic challenges. Individuals with penchants for reframing problems and customizing solutions deserve a special place in your department.

This question should not disintegrate into a bragging session whereas the interviewee feels compelled to list point by point what she has accomplished. Rather, it is a good opening to discern to what extent the candidate values collegiality and the ability to get along with colleagues.

Question 2: Every Department Has Its Own "Dysfunctionality Quotient." In Your Last Position, What Were the Quirks and How Did You Deal with Them?

Tolerance for a department's shortcomings and inconsistencies is definitely an area that calls for compatible personality styles. Signs of dysfunction within a department include an overactive grapevine, jealousy, a deterioration of department ethics, courses not being taught, not attaining resources (for example, traveling to conferences, graduate assistants, and so on), and cynicism. Every department shares these characteristics at any given time—only the *degree* of dysfunctionality varies. Engaging a candidate to objectively address these department weaknesses demands that the individual ride a fine line between outright, subjective criticism and an objective, evaluative critique of organizational shortcomings.

This question enables the search committee to assess the candidate's insights into the problems he has faced battling bureaucracy as well as the solutions he has provided in attempting to overcome those departmental flaws. If a candidate places himself in a victim posture by identifying weaknesses that negatively affected his performance, then beware of this person's capacity for dealing with adversity. As long as there are people in a department within a university, there will be personality conflicts, power plays, weak leaders, jealous peers, and apathetic subordinates. Placing blame on the department for not controlling these universally human issues spells weakness on the candidate's part.

Question 3: In What Areas Do You Typically Have the Least Amount of Patience in Working with Your Fellow Faculty Members?

This personal question is important in view of the fact that relationships are as intimate as the collegial alliance between and among faculty members—tenured as well as nontenured.

Typically, candidates will shy away from addressing situations that try their patience because there is simply nothing to gain by offering a truthful response. After all, they are supposed to be patient with their chairs, deans, students, and peers all the time. Period. Many candidates will speak solely about their impatience with their own performance, thereby avoiding placing blame on anyone else. Others will raise acceptable issues regarding their impatience with coworkers who feel entitled to a job or to job security just because they show up at the university every day.

A strategy for getting more mileage out of this question is to ask follow-up questions such as these:

"What is it like working with you? What should we expect on a day-to-day basis?"

"What would your response be if a senior, tenured faculty member in our department seems to be against everything you try to do and accomplish?"

Question 4: If We Were to Ask Your Colleagues to Describe Your Strengths and Weaknesses in Communicating with Other Faculty Members, Students, and Management, What Would They Say?

Communication skills are very important in enhancing the climate of any work environment. This is especially true in universities where some people in a department are tenured and some are not. The search committee can further assess this by speaking with a candidate's former employer.

A common response may be that a candidate will say, "I get along with others and I am very well liked and respected by my peers." The job of the search committee will be to add some concrete critical mass to this response by asking further probing questions such as these:

> "Tell me about the last time you became 'unwound' while dealing with coworkers. What tried your patience or caused your anger?"

> "Have you ever found it necessary to show your anger and not back down in a confrontation with other faculty members, students, or management?"

> "Give me an example of the most irrational, rude, and intimidating peer faculty member you had to deal with at your last position. How did you handle the situation? In retrospect, how could you have handled it differently?"

Question 5: Tell Us About a Conflict You Had with a Colleague in the Past That, Looking Back, You Would Have Handled Differently.

Confronting problem colleagues is daunting for even the most confident faculty members. Some take a direct, unequivocal approach in delivering constructive criticism. Others provide a light and tactful touch and couch criticism in a context of warranted praise for work well done.

Recognize that very few people will describe their primary means of dealing with conflict as an avoidance of confrontation (no backbone) or their hot-headed tendencies (perceived as reckless, undisciplined, and tactless). The ability to look back, with hindsight being 20–20, will offer more balanced insight into this touchy but critical issue. Candidates should be afforded an opportunity to paint a picture of the circumstances and explain the necessity for taking a strong course of action.

The word *conflict* should be carefully critiqued. A candidate is asked to indicate a specific situation that brought about conflict, analyze the circumstances surrounding the conflict, and think through how it could have been handled differently. Even the best of candidates would opt to change history if given the chance. The search committee should look for solutions in the candidate's response that show creativity and ingenuity in reframing the problem issue and its outcomes.

It is important that the candidate not perseverate and blame peers and students for any discomfort in relations at their last position. Also, if there were interpersonal problems the two key areas to look for in candidate responses focus on (1) what the candidate learned from the incident and (2) how willing the person was to accept responsibility for her actions. Both are earmarks of a person's maturity and reflect well on a candidate's objective self-evaluation skills.

Question 6: All of Us Have Core Principles, Values, or Beliefs That We View as Nonnegotiable. What Issues Would Cause You to "Go to the Mat"?

Differences in opinion are inevitable; conflict is optional. You want faculty members who stand up for themselves. But you do not want someone who is too eager to draw lines in the sand and prepare for battle over every little thing. If the instincts of the search committee are that you are getting less than the whole story, probe further regarding specific instances in which the candidate stuck to her guns, no matter what.

Candidates may feel challenged by this inquiry because respondents are forced to defend their actions unilaterally and pit themselves against the people with whom they work. Still, this question will surface extreme issues at the margin of that person's work history, namely, disagreement and disharmony with a colleague. Although we hope that such conflict is rare, it will inevitably face a department one day if you hire this person, so it is useful to find out how she dealt with it in the past.

If the true nature of the faculty member–faculty member relationship lies in complementing each others' strengths and weaknesses, then the search committee will want to find a faculty member who wants to keep the peace and who is able to maintain an objective perspective even in view of an all-out victory.

Hiring a peacemaker makes a great deal of sense when your goal for the department is to maintain positive interpersonal relations with the staff. People who are at ease with themselves and keep an objective distance from the action will offer a rationale sounding board to their faculty peers even when emotions are high. In the final analysis, it is not who's right or wrong; it is how the inevitable conflict gets resolved. The fewer the emotional battles and histrionics, the better. Long-standing feuds over who "won" and who "lost" can render a department dysfunctional!

Question 7: Which of the Following Three Factors Would Play the Most Significant Role in Your Decision to Accept the Offer from This Institution: (1) the University, (2) the Position You Are Applying For, or (3) the People You Would Be Working With?

It is important to ask candidates to confirm why joining your department makes sense for them from a career or personal standpoint. The answer will allow the search committee to determine the "homework" the person has done concerning the university (for example, its culture, mission, and so on), the specific faculty position (for example, teaching load, research and publication expectations, and so on), and the other faculty members in the department (for example, reputation of colleagues, expertise of faculty members, and so on) (Falcone, 2008).

A search committee may elect to ask candidates only one or two of these seven questions. The questions are designed to measure collegiality but not to be overly prescriptive in that all seven must be asked. Interview committees can decide which, if any, are the most germane for their purpose.

Problem

CASE STUDY

You are the chair of a department of fifteen full-time faculty members. You have a large number of students majoring in your department. You also teach four sections of an all-university-required course each semester. After many years of advocating for another full-time faculty position, your dean has indicated that you can hire one new person at the assistant or associate professor level. You are fearful that if you do not hire one of the two finalists you will lose this much-needed position. Each of the two finalists has worked at two other universities for a combined total of nine years. Following are the candidates' qualifications as indicated by their CVs and what you found out by reaching out to people they have worked with:

Candidate A

- Average teacher
- Great researcher
- "Tolerates" students
- Great grant getter
- Widely respected in your field for cutting-edge research
- Terrible colleague

Candidate B

- Good teacher
- Does not publish
- Known in your field and liked by peers
- Liked by students

- Never has written a grant
- Great colleague

So, whom do you hire?

Possible Solution

Perhaps your decision will be predicated on the type of institution in which you work; for example, a Research 1 university will probably have different needs than another type of institution. Possibly you are a staunch believer in the Southwest Airlines slogan, "Hire for attitude and train for skill." Also, your past experiences can significantly influence your decision; for example, in the past you were witness to how one "terrible, toxic colleague" ruined the department. However, the best decision may be to have a failed search and start over again until you find a truly great candidate. After all, it is not fair to the candidate to hire him knowing that he will probably not gain tenure. It is also not fair to your students, your faculty colleagues, and the department as a whole to hire a person who clearly does not appear to fit into the department culture and climate.

Developing Codes for Collegial Conduct

Chairs, with the consensus of faculty members within the department, can develop specific rules and regulations that can enhance collegial behavior of students and faculty alike. It is strongly recommended that the chair encourages input by all faculty members in developing and implementing the codes that follow.

Developing a Department Code of Conduct

Buller (2006) wrote that "one way to work through the issues of collegiality is for a department to attempt to define a code of acceptable behavior" (p. 51). Such a code, adapted from Buller, might look like this:

> As members of the X department, we undertake to communicate with others, both orally and in writing, in a manner that is polite, respectful, civil, and courteous. Whenever we disagree with someone, we restrict our differences to the issue itself while continuing to respect the individual with whom we disagree. We agree to disagree without being disagreeable! We strongly encourage productive dissent by all members of our department. All of our discussion and argumentation will be conducted in a polite, courteous, civil, and dignified manner.

Most department and universities have a code of conduct for their *students* designed to bring civility to our classrooms . . . perhaps it is time to have one for our faculty members, staff, and administrators as well.

Student Code of Conduct

Incivility on the part of students can heighten tensions within the department. This may cause a cyclical response by faculty members and staff and serve to undermine the culture of civility, collegiality, and respect that you as chair are trying to develop and sustain. A student code of conduct such as this may be used:

> As a student majoring in the X department at YZ University, I understand that when I communicate with faculty members and students, both orally and in writing, that I should do so in a manner that is polite, respectful, civil, and courteous. Whenever I disagree with someone, I restrict our differences to the issue(s) itself while continuing to respect the individual with whom I disagree. This civil response is a basic tenet of attending our university. I agree to disagree without being disagreeable. All of my discussion and argumentation with faculty and fellow students

will be conducted in a polite, courteous, civil, and dignified manner.

Student _____ Date_____

Academic Honesty Statement

A department chair is often called on to mediate a problem between a student and a faculty member. The disposition of this problem, especially if the chair rules in favor of a student, can invoke an angry backlash from the faculty member. One of the most frequent problems that arise between a student and a faculty member is one of plagiarism. The following example shows one way that this potential conflict can be proactively dealt with:

As a student in the X department, I have been informed of the university and department policy on academic honesty and am aware of its availability in the YZ University student handbook. I fully understand plagiarism and its implications for my academic work as a student in the X department and YZ University. Further, I understand any errors, omissions, misrepresentations, or falsifications of source materials in any of my courses, if verified by a professor or his or her authorized representative, can and will be considered plagiarism by the instructor, department, school, and university, which may result in one or more of the following:

- A failing grade on an assignment
- A failing grade in a course
- Possible dismissal from the course
- Possible dismissal from the department consistent with X department policy

With my signature below, I hereby knowingly and willingly attest that I will abide by the X department expectation that any work I submit is honest and truthful and I further attest that what

I submit in any of my classes is my own work. I sign below freely of my own volition fully understanding the terms of this academic honesty statement.

Student _____ Date_____

"Department chairs should receive specific training, as part of ongoing chairs' support, concerning the steps one should take when addressing uncivil faculty behavior. These ideas should also be written into a department chair handbook, as well. Chairs should also have the opportunity to have department chair 'roundtable discussions' periodically throughout the semester when confidential discussions about these problems could transpire. Case studies could be used as a vehicle to address effective and ineffective strategies when dealing with uncivil behavior."
—Stuart J. Schleien, professor and director of graduate study, Department of Recreation, Tourism, and Hospitality Management, University of North Carolina at Greensboro

Council of Academic Chairs

It is useful for chairs to have peers readily available to discuss certain happenings at their university, to converse about specific elements of their position, to share ideas and solutions to common challenges, or merely to discuss general topics. Ideally, these peers will be chairs at the same university. The demands of all chairs are similar: reports will need to be handed in at the same time and the campus culture is somewhat the same. These peers can, individually and collectively, provide insight into myriad duties and responsibilities that are unique and distinct to being a department chair. This mutual support structure can aid chairs tremendously.

Southern Connecticut State University has established a Council of Academic

Chairs (CAC) that includes the chairs of each of the thirty-six departments in the university.

Bylaws of Southern Connecticut State University's Council of Academic Chairs

I. PURPOSE

Academic department chairs provide indispensable leadership and service to the university. The Council of Academic Chairs (CAC) will promote synergy among department chairs and efficacy in the performance of the chair role resulting in important gains for the university. The council will also work to develop structures for chairs and avenues for collective expression by chairs.

II. GOALS

1. Promote role definition of the department chair at SCSU.
2. Provide a mutual support structure for department chairs.
3. Enhance efficiency and effectiveness in the function of department chairs.
4. Provide a forum for consultation on affairs that concern department chairs.
5. Foster collective advocacy by department chairs for appropriate administrative and academic procedures.

III. MEMBERSHIP

The membership shall consist of chairs of academic departments.

(continued)

(*continued*)

IV. MEETINGS

The council shall schedule three (3) meetings per academic semester. Special meetings may be called on request of 10 percent of the membership.

V. ORGANIZATION

A facilitator will be elected for a one-year term. The facilitator will be responsible for developing and distributing an agenda. A member will be appointed secretary on a voluntary basis for each year. The secretary will be responsible for recording and distributing minutes and other pertinent materials.

*   *   *

The CAC has afforded chairs to come together and problem solve on a variety of common concerns and issues. It has grown into a powerful political as well as academic force on campus. The CAC devotes one meeting per semester at which the provost joins with the chairs to explain and discuss current and emerging trends and to answer any questions. The chair position at SCSU turns over at the rate of 20 to 25 percent per year (seven to nine new chairs). The council trains new chairs in myriad roles and responsibilities they will be expected to perform. Also, both formal and informal mechanisms have developed that allow new chairs to be mentored by more-seasoned chairs. However, there is a possible drawback to the CAC in which a small number of chairs are allowed the freedom to dominate the meeting complaining about everything and everyone: efforts should be made to make certain that the CAC does not disintegrate into a gripe session in which individuals are allowed to endlessly vent personal frustrations. In the final analysis, the CAC remains a viable entity for department chairs.

"COMPLAINT FREE ZONE"

Buller (2006) indicates that chairs should "work with your faculty members to develop a more positive philosophy of solving problems" (p. 63). He recommends that the department develop a statement along the following lines:

"Complaint-Free Zone"

As members of the X department, we seek to work together positively for the solution of problems and the resolution of conflicts. Rather than complaining or being disrespectful, we are interested in solutions to problems. We attempt to determine a plan of action that we ourselves can take to improve a situation and then we put that plan into effect. Rather than assuming the worst of others, we take it for granted that every member of the department and of YZ University as a whole is working toward the good of our students. Rather than becoming preoccupied with the faults of others, we prefer to focus on their strengths, providing positive and constructive mentoring to the best of our abilities.

Conclusion

Two of the most important decisions universities make are whom to hire and whom to tenure. It will be advantageous for departments to assess potential faculty members regarding collegiality before they are hired.

Chairs fully recognize that lack of collegiality can lead to a department's demise. A chair should express this fact to all members in the department. The chair should address the meaning as well as the value of collegiality at an open department meeting. Collegiality will be operationally defined and examples of collegiality (for example, collaboration, treating everyone with respect, compassion, and tact, and so on) and noncollegiality (for example, nasty comments, flaming e-mails, personal attacks, and so on) will be discussed in a transparent and non-threatening way. Consensus should be gained and everyone should buy into the concept of the values inherent in sustaining a collegial department. Most people in institutions of higher education are cognizant of the fact that there is an inevitability of conflict. The department, led by the chair, should formulate formal procedures for managing conflict. The department should strive to be a pillar of the university; a department that respects students, professional staff, colleagues, and peers and a place where people are proud to work and study.

Chapter Three provides the reader with relevant and useful informational materials designed to help the chair facilitate a collegial department.

3

STRATEGIES FOR PROMOTING COLLEGIALITY

> You can accomplish anything in life, provided that
> you do not mind who gets the credit.
> > —*Harry S. Truman (McCullough, 1992)*

I am no longer mystified by the fact that two departments seemingly identical in their composition and demographics are completely disparate in their climate. Each department may have eight faculty members, 150 student majors, and approximately the same composite make-up of the rest of the faculty (age, ethnicity, and educational levels); however, one department is enthusiastic, collaborative, and intellectual (faculty members clearly enjoy coming to work) and the other department is isolated, deadening, and depressing (faculty members stay away as much as possible—they unmistakably dislike coming to work). The salient difference may be that one department faculty member treats his fellow faculty colleagues in demeaning, degrading, noncollegial, disrespectful, and uncivil ways. The chair and dean are unable or unwilling to put an end to this dystopia. Lack of civility and collegiality can deleteriously affect the department, its students, professional staff, and other faculty members.

There are many departments that suffer from noncollegial, disrespectful, uncivil, and nasty encounters between faculty members, chair and faculty members, faculty members and staff, and faculty members and students. And, by a process of elimination, the chair must deal with all of them on a regular basis.

Department chairs are led to believe that that is merely the way it is, that they must struggle on their own to deal with a non-collegial and downright nasty faculty member or a department culture in which civility is compromised. However, there are proved strategies that chairs can employ to put a halt to this noncollegial and uncivil behavior. A department chair can take proactive steps to stem the tide of noncollegiality by recognizing its telltale signs in the department:

- Low morale in the department
- No collaboration between and among faculty members
- Poor student advisement
- No department celebrations or social alliances
- Office doors remain closed—whether faculty member is in or out
- More classes being cancelled—faculty members not showing up to teach their class
- Faculty office hours not kept
- High turnover by faculty—young, untenured faculty leave the university entirely
- Increased early retirements
- Increased absenteeism and tardiness
- Diminished work quality of once-productive faculty
- New faculty struggling to survive
- Older, more seasoned faculty worn down and becoming disengaged from the department and the institution
- A culture manifested by a lugubrious state of mind
- Communication within the department described as inchoate
- Urban legends of the department's past glory take on an appearance of verisimilitude
- Increased illness and health issues

- Working from home more than usual or more than necessary
- Lower or poorer work quality
- Increasing faculty isolation and alienation
- Low degree of meaningful faculty participation in governance activities
- Poor faculty performance patterns
- Low research productivity
- Poor teaching evaluations from students and peers
- More student complaints (about teaching, meeting classes, advising, attitude of professor, not holding office hours, and so on)
- Lack of or minimal attendance to scheduled faculty meetings
- Refusal to serve on department, school, or university committees
- Consistency of poor faculty evaluations

A positive change in the culture of the department will either be white blood cells that will heal the department or, if allowed to remain unchanged, continue to persist as malignant cells that will continue to sap its strength.

Question: "How would you handle a situation in which the department has already established a poor climate? What steps can a college or university take once things go wrong?"

* * *

Answer: "This is a *very* difficult challenge. It is far better to be proactive. However, there are probably long-standing feuds that have turned personal and toxic. I strongly suggest that a formal intervention strategy be developed—the sooner the better. Note: as a general rule, 'informal' is more effective. In this case, however, a formal strategy is required.

(continued)

(*continued*)

I further suggest that an outside person—certainly outside the department but probably from outside the university—be brought in to meet with the department members. This person should have expertise in managing conflict. This outside person will fact-find, meet with individual faculty members as well as the entire department as a group, and develop an agreed-on strategy to restore collegiality, respect, and civility in the department." —Robert E. Cipriano, professor emeritus, Department of Recreation and Leisure Studies, Southern Connecticut State University

The Chair's Role in Facilitating a Collegial Department

Mary Lou Higgerson (1996) has written about strategies to be employed by department chairs to develop collegial relationships in a department. In addition, I have found the following twenty leadership traits that chairs can use to help facilitate a more collegial department:

- *Emphasize consensus.* Chairs should work tirelessly to gain buy-in from members of their department. This enhances a sense of empowerment as well as the fact that encouraging more ideas and suggestions—delivered in a respectful and civil manner—is a basic tenet of institutions of higher education.
- *Share power.* Chairs should not be power-hungry and driven by their egos. They should reach out to the faculty members and obtain their thoughts and ideas. Faculty members should recognize that the chair makes decisions predicated on the needs of the department, not personal gain.

- *Consult with all faculty members.* Chairs should not be perceived as listening only to one or two faculty members. When people are listened to, and their ideas are allowed to be articulated, they are empowered.

- *Develop and implement shared responsibilities.* Chairs should be aware that all faculty members must share the workload. Resist giving most of the work to a small minority of the faculty—even if they are not tenured! There should be equity in committee assignments, number of advisees, and so on.

- *De-emphasize status differences.* Chairs should help to ensure that senior-ranking professors and first-year faculty members are accorded the same respect. Institutions of higher education are infamous for heightening status differences. Quality departments must refrain from this position.

- *Individuals should interact as equals.* Chairs must set the tone and be certain that all people in the department are treated as equals. The chair must model the behavior she expects from faculty members, students, and professional staff.

- *Engage in generational and gender equity.* Chairs should ensure that more seasoned faculty and women and minorities are respected and listened to. The composition of faculty is changing and chairs need to recognize this.

- *Celebrate.* Chairs should celebrate, publicly and privately, the achievements of each faculty member: awarding of tenure, promotion in rank, writing a grant, writing an article for publication, obtaining a grant or contract, awarded the "best" researcher or teacher or advisor honor, and so on.

- *Maintain frequent and consistent interaction with colleagues.* Hold weekly, regularly scheduled staff meetings. The chairs who interact with their staff mainly through e-mails are doing themselves and the department a disservice.

- *Establish a climate of tolerating differences.* Higher education is rather infamously noted for harboring people who display idiosyncratic behavior. Department climate should encourage a dissimilarity and variation in ideas and thoughts by faculty members.

- *Focus on the behavior not the person.* In discussions that become heated, as well as normal exchanges between and among faculty members and the chair, it is the behavior that should be carefully scrutinized rather than the person.

- *Be constructive and informative.* The chair is in a position to be more informed than faculty members regarding important changes underway at the college or university. The chair should present as much of this information as logic would dictate so that faculty members are spared the insidious rumors that often accompany impending changes. The chair should communicate what he knows to the faculty in a positive, practical, and useful way.

- *Link individuals to the larger context.* If a person makes an ill-advised uncivil comment one time, it should not be blown out of proportion as representing a declaration that this is her usual behavior. We all have bad days. However, if this becomes a noticeable occurrence it must be dealt with, and swiftly.

- *Do not be defensive: "I'm not being defensive, damn it!"* It is human nature that when one starts a sentence with the phrase "Don't be defensive, but . . ." the immediate response is to declare that you are not! Try not to start off a conversation with this expression.

- *Publicly and formally recognize each deserving person.* A faculty member should be recognized when he or she performs in an outstanding way. The chair should take the lead in making sure that the person's achievement does not go unrecognized or unnoticed. The chair can organize a breakfast or lunch to honor this person's success. He can make an announcement at a department or schoolwide meeting. The important thing is to recognize this person and her achievement in a public forum.

- *Clarify performance expectations.* The chair should meet individually with each faculty member at the start of each semester and discuss performance expectations. The expectations will be somewhat different and unique for each faculty member, based on where each faculty member is in his or her career. Of course, a tenured full professor will have a different set of goals and expectations than a nontenured assistant professor. This will enable chairs to get to know their faculty members, obtain information on their dreams and aspirations, and mentor the faculty members in specific ways.

- *Be consistent.* Chairs should behave in a consistent manner so that faculty members, students, and professional staff are secure in their interaction with the chair. This behavior can serve as a reliability check to ensure that the chair is not behaving sporadically from day to day. Each person in the department should be noticeably comfortable in daily relations with the chair.

- *Keep accurate, specific, and up-to-date records.* The chair should keep records of communications he has, especially those that are contentious. He should record the time and day of the conversation and the outcome. The records should be kept in a secure place and labeled properly for easy reference.

- *Do not show favoritism.* Even the perception that the chair is favoring one faculty person over another sets in motion needless conflict. Faculty members have elephantine memories! Chairs should be ever-vigilant in not making the "favoritism game" into a self-fulfilling prophecy. I have always shared the decisions that I have made with all of the members in the department. For example, Jim was supported in attending a national conference, while Ellen's request was denied. The reason that I shared was that Jim was presenting a keynote address at the conference. Also, Ellen was requesting to go to the conference and only attend the sessions. Jim's keynote presentation brought acclaim to the department and the university. Morning classes usually begin at 8:00 AM. Faculty members do not want to teach the eight o'clock class. The decision I made was to rotate the faculty so that we all (myself included) taught the 8:00 AM class every fifth semester.

- *Resist the temptation to get even and punish a faculty member (even if he is a mean-spirited son-of-a-sea cook)*. Chairs must personally defend against placing a faculty member in a dark, windowless, asbestos-filled office in the basement of the maintenance building. Although this may provide the chair with a warm and fuzzy feeling, she should refrain from actually doing this or similar acts (it is okay, however, to think it). Punishing this person makes the chair seem petty and vindictive in the eyes of other faculty members, students, and staff. Also, it only serves to set this person up as a victim. Faculty members do have an innate tendency to relate to victims, which could serve to ostracize the chair and significantly diminish her effectiveness as a leader.

Question: "What can or should a chair do to facilitate a more collegial and civil department?"

* * *

Answer: "Let faculty members know it is the most important thing to having a successful department and that incivility will not be tolerated. They could also say, if their administration approves this, that incivility is grounds for dismissal." —Susan Hannam, dean, College of Health, Environment and Science, Slippery Rock University

Answer: "This could be done by having the faculty set rules of behavior and asking all to indicate their support and endorsement. This sets group expectations. If a tenure-track faculty member is not civil, each instance must be documented. When multiple events take place these can be part of the annual review process when correct behavior can be raised as a mechanism to avoid sanctions. For nontenure-track faculty members there is the nonreappointment mechanism after due process. In cases in which sanctions may be indicated after discussion, warnings, and other interventions, the support of upper administration is essential. They should be informed of potential cases from the outset."
—Douglas Lees, professor emeritus, Department of Biology, Indiana State University–Purdue University Indianapolis

Answer: "Develop ground rules or acceptable behaviors agreed on by the department members. Address the expectations of departmental behaviors at a department retreat or setting with sufficient time to work as a group. Create the expectation that the department chair must move from a 'collection of scholars' to a 'community of scholars.' Work with other department chairs, maybe as a volunteer council of chairs, to share ideas and support each other in developing a sense of department team." —Walter H. Gmelch, dean, School of Education, University of San Francisco

Answer: "First and foremost, a chair must confront the faculty member and discuss his or her inappropriate actions. Also, departmental, school, and university expectations for civil and appropriate behavior within the department should be reviewed at this time. I would also direct the individual toward an appropriate supportive service, on campus, if the faculty member wishes to seek help at that time. It is important to have this meeting as early as possible, with uncivil

(*continued*)

(*continued*)

behavior not left to fester throughout the term or academic year. As we all know, left to its own course, uncivil behavior can become cancerous and transition into an ineffective team of faculty (and students). This session must be documented in writing and placed in the faculty member's personnel file. I recommend that the discussion and documentation be shared with the dean, as well." —Stuart J. Schleien, professor and director of graduate study, Department of Recreation, Tourism, and Hospitality Management, University of North Carolina at Greensboro

Answer: "As to what the chair can do: this depends on whether the chair has the respect of the faculty or not."
—Jerry G. Chmielewski, chairperson, Department of Biology, Slippery Rock University

Answer: "I would first attempt to discuss the issue with the faculty member. My goal would be to make sure that he or she understands what it means to be collegial and what the expectations for collegial behavior are. Fortunately, our university has a collegiality policy, which assists in clarifying what collegiality is and is not. I would also want to be sure that the faculty member is aware of the university collegiality policy. I would meet with the faculty member again (perhaps two to three times depending on the severity of the transgression[s]) and would then file a formal complaint under the collegiality policy of the university." —Sue Ouellette, chair, Department of Communicative Disorders, Northern Illinois University

Practical Advice Chairs Can Pursue

Coffman (2005) shared that the chair plays an important role in creating a positive department climate, one "that allows for productive dissent, raw debate, and reasoned discourse, but mitigates unproductive conflict and disputes . . . through the al-location of work, the annual goal setting and evaluation and re-ward process, and also by adding the right personal touch day to day. . . . the chair must know the strengths, weaknesses, and aspirations of every member of her faculty" (p. 77).

Buller (2006) wrote that "every department chair under-stands the importance of promoting collegiality within his or her department. Few factors can bring the productivity of a de-partment to a standstill and destroy its reputation as quickly as can the presence of even a single uncollegial faculty member. Continued breaches of collegiality have been known to destroy departmental morale, alienate capable students, cost the depart-ment some of its most valued faculty members, and decrease a department's competitiveness when it applies for grants and other forms of external support" (p. 50).

Chu (2006) stated that "chairs are the frontline officers charged with protecting the rights of those in the department and seeing to it that unethical and immoral behavior does not occur on their watch" (p. 76). He made the following recom-mendations that chairs should consider when dealing with chal-lenging people in the department:

- "Consult human resources" (p. 77). In fact, I will add that chairs should make use of any and all resources within their institution. I have called on colleagues in the departments of counseling and school psychology, marriage and family therapy, and special education to assist me in both understanding a person's behavior and to have them actually meet with our department to serve as mediators and facilitators in resolving the asperity in the department. Chairs should not act alone; there are a great many resources that they can, and should, use from within their institution.

- "Make sure your dean knows what is going on" (p. 77). The dean should always be included in the loop. Chairs should keep their dean fully informed because (1) the dean should never be surprised and caught off guard and (2) the problem(s) may find their way to the dean or beyond the dean to the offices of central administration. A first-rate dean can also provide counsel to the chair and call on additional resources that the institution has at its disposal.

- Have individual discussions with challenging personnel to get their point of view. "No matter how difficult it may be, chairs need to arrange personal individual discussions with the problematic faculty or staff member and those negatively affected by that person" (p. 77).

- "Build a case" (p.77). Any actions taken against a person require a substantial amount of evidence showing a consistent pattern of aberrant behavior over time. The chair must document with objective evidence those behaviors in violation of established institutional policy. The chair should elicit documentation from all people who have witnessed the inappropriate behavior.

- Bolster your defenses. "If you decide that your department has a problem that requires action, prepare to be attacked" (p. 79). The chair should gain the support of the dean, central administration, and her colleagues in the department and throughout campus. Every college or university has its own unique blend of political reality and power bases. The chair should proactively reach out to these key stakeholders for support and advice.

These descriptions represent proved strategies that chairs can follow when faced with an uncollegial faculty member. However, merely following a prescribed approach to enhancing collegiality does not, in and of itself, ensure its success. It is my fervent conviction that two department chairs can subscribe to these principles but have very different results, predicated on the amount of trust and respect the chair has generated on the part of the faculty. The remainder of this chapter will cogitate on these concepts and explore ubiquitous personal characteristics that the chair already possesses or can learn to acquire.

Proactive Strategies Chairs Can Employ to Promote Collegiality in the Department

This spring I reread *Atlas Shrugged* by Ayn Rand. This novel, one of the most influential business books ever written, was published more than fifty years ago, on October 12, 1957. Rand glorified the right of individuals to live entirely for their own interests. She staunchly defended personal success. John Galt was the hero who ascribed to this lifestyle in Rand's twelve-hundred-page work of fiction.

Do faculty members in higher education subscribe to this self-interested concept? Where are the John Galts among the faculty? Perhaps there are more of them than we imagine. Faculty members, like people in all industries, strive to be rewarded for their efforts. In business and industry, people are compensated for their productive work by bonuses, free vacations to exotic places, and other financially driven incentives. People in the academy have a different set of rewards and, by contrast, punishments that are inherent and vastly distinct to institutions of higher education. Academicians strive for promotion in rank—from assistant to associate to full professor. They endeavor to be reappointed each year prior to their obtaining tenure. They also compete for merit pay increases—albeit, the financial rewards are relatively meager. However, it does serve to stroke the ego and provide a personal basis of comparison (that is, a scorecard of how one is doing compared with peers). In higher education, Rand's deification of the right of individuals to live for their own interests culminates in the ultimate utopian reward, the holy grail of academe, tenure!

Destructive conflict can ruin once-great departments. The department chair is often the person who is called on to intervene when a person is uncivil, disrespectful, and noncollegial to others in the department. It is certainly much easier to not re-appoint a person who displays a consistent pattern of noncolle-gial behavior during the typical six-year probation time before a tenure decision is made. The U.S. courts have indicated (see Chapter Seven) that they will not protect uncivil faculty and that a person's noncollegial behavior is a legitimate reason not to reappoint him. This seems like a nonparlous way to rid a de-partment of a toxic person. A word of caution: the chair must be mindful that objective documentation is needed in order to pur-sue this approach. My experience as a long-standing department chair, as well as numerous conversations with my peers across the country, is that nontenured assistant professors are not likely to cause a kerfuffle in the department. They fully realize that they have not obtained the rewards associated with higher edu-cation, namely, promotion to the rank of associate or full profes-sor and tenure. What strategies can the chair employ when most of the carrots have been awarded? How can the chair beseech and cajole senior tenured faculty to behave in a civil, respectful, and collegial way?

In the course of a single day, the chair is called on to make decisions that directly affect members of the department as well as have the potential to spill over into a personal war if the deci-sion does not favor a particular person. Some decisions are seem-ingly harmless: "Dr. Dudas, we will have to raise the maximum number of students in your Bio 100 class from fifteen to seven-teen." Other decisions are seemingly more fraught with the potential for conflict: "Dr. Brookshire, students have told me you are not meeting your classes regularly." The reactions of the affected faculty members may be quite different than what one would expect. Dr. Dudas reacts by aiming a profane fusillade at the chair. Dr. Brookshire apologizes and states how sorry she is and ensures the chair that this will not happen again. The responses may be based primarily on the respect and credibility that the chair has within the department. How the department chair is viewed by faculty members, students, and administrators will oftentimes determine if there will be a flashpoint for jump starting a climate fraught with detritus and asperity. So how does the chair proactively gain the respect needed to facilitate a collegial department so that it does not descend into Hummer-like inefficiency?

First and foremost, a chair must recognize that people do not respond to your "techniques." People respond to your values—who you are. I have already noted that more than 96 percent of chairs have not been trained or educated in myriad duties that they are expected to perform (Cipriano and Riccardi, 2010). In addition, more than 81 percent of chairs surveyed in the same study indicated that character, integrity, and trustworthiness were essential skills they needed to possess to be effective.

In order to establish the required ingredients for a positive culture and climate to exist in the department, the chair must model the characteristics she wishes the faculty and staff to exhibit. The "do as I say not as I do" pattern is fraught with distrust and meaningless jargon. The chair must demonstrate respect, constantly and consistently, to all faculty members, professional staff, and students. Chairs should personally acknowledge that the department chair is a service position in which they should view themselves as equals rather than as galactic overlords. The following positive characteristics regarding how a chair is perceived by professional members of the department are rather obvious. The list includes those not previously mentioned. They can, most assuredly, help to facilitate a more collegial climate.

- Is highly visible (walks the halls rather than e-mails)
- Always available
- Humble
- Positive
- Transparent
- Consistent
- Shows appreciation

- A good listener
- Objective
- Has vision
- Has integrity
- Is motivated to get things done

When these characteristics are viewed in a more holistic and comprehensive system it becomes self-evident that they all reflect best practices in leadership. It is inarguable that a department chair must be a leader. However, because of myriad roles chairs are called on to demonstrate on a daily basis, I would add another, far-reaching concept that chairs can follow to facilitate a collegial department: invest in people.

Invest in People

Showing a genuine and caring interest in the well-being of the faculty, staff, and students can enhance the relationship between the chair and these key stakeholders. There are many ways in which department chairs can strive to show, by their words and actions, that they are truly invested in their welfare. Buller (personal communication, February 10, 2010) indicated that chairs should help people to achieve their goals. This shows that the chair has their best interests in mind and is willing to help people better themselves. This may be demonstrated by assisting a person in preparing documents for his tenure and promotion file, in helping a person to write an article or grant, or making concrete and valid recommendations to their teaching. To paraphrase Freiberg and Freiberg (1996), students and administrators come second; faculty members come first! A chair's credibility is enhanced ten-fold when her faculty know that she has their "back" and she supports them wholeheartedly. Logically, this will go a long way in establishing and sustaining a positive and constructive relationship with her staff. The department chair should also reflect on whether his actions match his stated values. Self-reflection is a necessary talent in self-improvement and one that will have far-reaching and long-lasting consequences. At the same time, a chair should build value in the people in his department. This value may be in the form of a mentoring relationship relative to skills the faculty member will need to be successful as well as personal values the person can employ (for example, have a balance in life; spend time with family; be collegial, civil, and respectful to your peers and colleagues; and so on). When you invest in people, you are empowering them: what a gift this is! The little things a chair does consistently—writing a handwritten note thanking a person for a job well done, verbally recognizing the person at a public meeting, sending a copy of her recently published article to the dean—means a great deal. It truly is not all about the salary!

If a chair is treated in a disrespectful way, he should not retaliate or respond in kind. Poor behavior by others does not require an insensitive response on the part of the chair. The person just might be having a bad day, and as long as this is not a consistent behavior on the person's part, it is better to not confront the person immediately. It should, however, be addressed as soon as feasible in a respectful and professional manner.

> "The art of being wise is the art of knowing what to overlook."
>
> —William James (1890)

When working closely with colleagues, it is important to realize that a person's attributes far outrank their surface credentials. This is especially true within institutions of higher education where the majority of faculty members have been awarded advanced graduate degrees. There also exists a rigid hierarchy whereby a full professor outranks his assistant professor colleague. Celebrate a person's birthday, an article written, a grant submitted, a positive tenure or promotion decision, the graduation of a faculty member's child, a "special" day (for example, the date the department was founded), holidays, a faculty member being recognized for an honor, going out to lunch together for no obvious reason, and so on. Celebrations create and enhance a sense of community. They also acknowledge those things that are important and valued and help build and cement relationships.

CASE STUDY

Problem

You are the department chair of a small but dynamic department consisting of six full-time faculty members. Two tenured associate professors in your department, Dr. Raffaela and Dr. Hatfield, each come to you and say that they do not want to teach a late evening class from 7:35 to 10:05 one night per week. You are afraid that whatever you do will harm the team esprit de corps of the department. What will you do?

- Decide who is right and ask the other person to go along with the decision.
- Wait and see; the best solution will become apparent.
- Tell both Drs. Raffaela and Hatfield not to get anxious; it is not that important.
- Get Drs. Raffaela and Hatfield together and examine both of their thoughts closely.
- Get the dean to make the decision.
- Think of another way to solve this dilemma.

Possible Solution

Your pre-established policy in the department is that all faculty rotate in teaching the late evening class. Your department offers one late class per semester, two per year. With six faculty members rotating in teaching the late evening class, each faculty member will be called on to teach the late evening class one time every three years. Therefore, it is Dr. Raffaela's turn to teach the class.

Conclusion

The challenges faced by all institutions of higher education in the twenty-first century cannot be successfully mastered or the effects of dedicated professionals sustained when attitudes and dispositions of personnel within departments are divisive, uncompromising, and inflexible or reflect a lesser degree of personal responsibility around a unified purpose. The chair should be cognizant of the fact that the most valuable assets in her department are the faculty members, the intellectual capital they possess, and the culture they create. Leadership is more a function of people's relationships than the position they occupy. Relationships built on trust, fed by personal integrity, and treating people with dignity and respect is well worth the time and effort and will go a very long way in promoting a collegial department.

Chapter Four discusses both negative and positive effects of conflict. The chapter also provides useful insights in turning a conflict into a problem to be managed.

4

MANAGING CONFLICT WITHIN THE DEPARTMENT

> If we could read the secret history of our enemies,
> we should find in each man's life sorrow and
> suffering enough to disarm all hostility.
> —*Henry Wadsworth Longfellow*

Conflict is inevitable. Being disrespectful and uncivil is a conscious choice. It is the result of competing ideas or options.

Positive Effects of Conflict

When most people merely hear the word *conflict* they associate a host of negative connotations. Peg Pickering (2000) discussed some positive consequences of conflict:

Increased motivation. The energy gained from a conflict situation escalates, adding stimulus to solving problems.

Enhanced problem identification. Conflict catalyzes thoughts and creates new opportunities.

Increased group cohesiveness. Working through conflict in a positive manner creates trust and increases productivity.

Reality adjustment. People in conflict are bounced out of their comfort zones and can view it as an opportunity for change.

Increased knowledge and skills.

Stimulates creativity. Conflict causes the consideration of new ideas.

Conflict stimulates three vital components for accomplishing goals:

- Thought
- Discussion
- Action

Incentives for growth. Conflict creates a learning situation. Conflict can also be constructive when it

- Identifies solutions to problems
- Results in a clarification of important problems, challenges, or issues
- Builds cooperation among the group
- Aids in *reducing* stress because challenges are brought into the open
- Energizes departments and relationships
- Benefits the group
- Clearly identifies power relationships within the department
- Encourages creativity and brainstorming
- Focuses on individual and group contributions rather than group decisions
- Brings emotive, nonrational arguments into the open
- Provides for catharsis—release of interdepartmental or interpersonal conflicts of long-standing duration
- Manages to yield constructive outcomes

These potential positive benefits to conflict cannot be realized, however, if the conflict is ignored or poorly handled. Just as it is true that you cannot work effectively with others with clenched fists, it is also true that you cannot smile conflict away; it must be managed. If conflict is not managed, it becomes detrimental or even destructive.

Negative Effects of Conflict

Pickering (2000) discussed these potential negative effects of conflict:

- Decreased productivity
- Erosion of trust
- Coalition formation with polarized positions
- Secrecy and reduced information flow
- Morale problems
- Consumption of mass amounts of time
- Decision-making paralysis

Conflict can also be destructive when it

- Interferes with other important activities
- Hinders productive output
- Obstructs goals and objectives in an organization
- Prevents members from "seeing" the task
- Dislocates the entire group and produces polarizations
- Subverts the objectives in favor of special interest subgoals
- Results in the disintegration of the entire group
- Stimulates win-lose conflicts in which reason is secondary to emotion
- Results in feuds that never end
- Results in disengagement
- Increases defensiveness
- Creates divisiveness
- Threatens effective problem solving and decision making
- Undermines good feelings and sense of camaraderie
- Fractures cohesiveness

- Polarizes positions
- Instills difficulty in seeking cooperation
- Forces colleagues to take sides

Chairs set the tone for a healthy climate and establishing and maintaining a positive culture in the department. As discussed in Chapter Three, if the chair is respected by members in the department, she has a far greater chance of quickly defusing destructive conflict in the department. When the department chair has an enviable track record of being trustworthy, of treating everyone with dignity and respect, and being honest and fair, it is easier to manage conflict. In higher education, we encourage disparate and contrasting viewpoints. When all sides of a problem are fully explored, when the discussions are civil and respectful, people are in a desirable position to make a quality decision. This can also serve to revivify a department.

Members of the academy are well versed in analytical thinking and are passionate in verbalizing their thoughts. Divergent thinking enhances the ability to find solutions to a problem. All people in the department—from graduate assistants up to and including full professors—should have opportunities to express their thoughts *respectfully* without fear of retaliation. A healthy, trustful climate in the department sets the tone for conducting department business in a constructive manner.

Conflict Summarized

We do know that conflict is inevitable—it is the natural outcome of human interaction. Anger, grudges, hurt, and blame are not inevitable. Incivility and lack of respect is chosen. Conflict occurs because of individual differences. Destructive conflict causes inefficiency. There are many reasons for departmental conflict to occur within institutions of higher education: jealousy, power, status, money, perceived hurts or slights, convenience, easy scapegoat, personality disorders, ghosts of the past ("I remember in 1981 . . . "), get-even time (finally), put the heat on him takes the heat off me, and equity issues ("Jim has a larger office or more windows in his office or a newer computer or went to a national conference."). Although conflict is to be expected, how we choose to respond is a choice.

Conflict can be *positive*. It can improve problem solving, clarify issues, increase participant involvement and commitment, and result in a better decision or outcome. Conflict can be *managed*. There are conflict-management skills and techniques that exist. Conflict resolution is not the same as conflict management. Chairs should not strive to resolve conflicts (even if we could) because a conflict-free environment would be one so homogeneous it could become not optimally innovative or productive. Problems will not go away by themselves.

The department chair plays a major and important role in managing conflict within the department. A chair's positive day-to-day interaction with faculty members, staff, and students can minimize destructive conflict. This daily interface can alert the chair to any cues that may signal a brewing conflict. Although chairs are not skilled in crystal-ball reading, they should be able to accurately predict potential conflicts and be ready to intervene when needed. This will be greatly facilitated if the chair walks the halls and interacts with faculty members, staff, and students on a daily basis.

Higgerson (1996) wrote that "if mutual trust exists among colleagues, and faculty air differences openly and constructively, there is less opportunity for destructive conflicts to escalate because individuals are less prone to perceive differences of opinion as personal attacks or components of some hidden agenda" (p. 142). Mutual respect and trust are significant cornerstones in facilitating an approach to managing conflict.

Sandra Cheldelin and Ann Lucas (2004) wrote that there are three conditions for interpersonal conflict to occur: "(1) some kind of expressed struggle between at least two parties, (2) these parties have an interdependent relationship, and (3) these parties perceive they are getting interference from each other in achieving their goals" (pp. 41–42). Managing a conflict is based on a clear understanding of what the dispute is really about. Good communication and engagement are keys to successfully managing conflict. When issues are not addressed quickly tension is heightened, resolution is delayed, and collateral damage is increased. The best approach to managing conflict is when the issues are handled in an informal way. In the final analysis, conflict management is directed toward reducing destructive conflict while allowing for the existence of constructive conflict. Communication, verbal and nonverbal, is the single most important ingredient to managing conflict.

Anger

Friends and colleagues have said to me that behind most conflicts, there is an outpouring of anger from at least one of the combatants. What do we really know about anger? What are the myths and realities?

- Getting angry is the only way to get things done.
- It is only natural to respond that way.
- Strongly confronting an angry person will back him or her down.
- Intimidation wins respect.
- Verbal or physical venting will have a lasting calming effect.
- Anger is a bad emotion.
- There is only one way to deal with anger.
- Anger can't be helped. ("This is just the way I am.")
- Not getting angry means they got away with it.
- Ignore it and it will go away.

These ten statements are *all myths*. In fact, getting angry is rarely the vehicle used to get anything done. It is clearly not natural to respond with uncontrolled anger and asperity. Confrontation and intimidation escalates situations so that it becomes a lose-lose proposition for all parties involved, including people on the periphery of the conflict. Verbal and physical venting is upsetting to all parties. Anger is not a bad emotion, per se. Anger can be kept under control, should not be parlous in nature, and the verbiage should not be delivered in a loud, acerbic, personal, and attacking way. The one-size-fits-all remedy does not exist to deal with anger. There are many proved ways that people can learn to deal with their anger that can change a potentially nasty confrontation into a civil discussion. Anger must be managed. Mishandled anger damages relationships and stifles teamwork.

Role of Department Chair

It is undeniable that chairs play a vital role in the culture and climate within their departments. If a chair has poor communication skills, appears to lack ownership or investment in his department, and portrays a perception that noncollegial and uncivil behavior are permitted, then he simply cannot lead his department.

Is a chair's self-image different from his or her perception by others? As a department chair, you should recognize that if you constantly fly off the handle your credibility will in all likelihood suffer. Chaos will reign in your department. Self-reflection is needed to determine what your "hot buttons" are and a game plan developed to avoid having your buttons pushed. Also, you should identify specific situations that trigger your hot buttons and think through scenarios that will help you to be prepared to respond tactfully and respectfully in these situations. More often than not a chair is placed in the middle of a heated exchange that is clearly escalating between two people. The chair is wise to buy time in this conflict so that she can respond with a level head. I have done this by asking the parties to reconvene at a mutually agreeable time. This allows people an opportunity to calm down and rationally think through the ramifications of their disagreement. A chair may, in a calm and soothing voice, ask questions that will help in understanding opposing views. A chair must be steadfast in his mind to actually want to deal with the situation, no matter how complicated, emotional, or difficult it may be.

In my career as a department chair I have had occasion to work with most of the following types of people:

- *The know-it-alls.* They have an arrogant demeanor and an opinion on every issue. They become defensive when they are proved to be wrong.
- *The excuse artists.* They have ready-made explanations for not completing an assignment, for missing their classes, for missing a department meeting, . . . for everything.
- *The intimidators.* They coerce, threaten, and bully people to get their way.
- *The passives.* They never offer ideas or never let you know their thoughts on any topic.
- *The dictators.* They bully and intimidate. They are constantly demanding and brutally critical.
- *The minimalists.* They absolutely do the minimum amount of work to get by. They are unique in their ability to understand what is considered a dereliction of their job responsibilities and do only a shade more above that.
- *The "yes" people.* They agree to any and all commitments, yet rarely if ever deliver on their promises. They hardly ever follow through on any task.
- *The "no" people.* They are "experts" at knowing why something will not work. These inflexible individuals wear down the rest of the group with their negativity.
- *The gripers.* Nothing is ever right with them. "It's too hot in here" (11:00 A.M.), "It's too cold in here" (11:01 A.M.).

Their preference is to complain rather than to think through solutions.

These different types of people certainly challenge you on an everyday basis! There are, however, ways to deal with specific kinds of difficult people. Your body language (that is, nonverbal communication) can be even more powerful than what you say. Only 7 percent of communication is actually transmitted verbally (Pickering, 2004). The remaining 93 percent is nonverbal. Facial expressions, body language, and the tone of voice all play a significant role in our conversations with others. The manner in which you position your body tells others how available you are to interact with and how interested you are in what they have to say.

"You can observe a lot by watching."
—Lawrence Peter ("Yogi") Berra (2003)

You can diffuse anger by practicing the following:

- Model the behavior you want the person to exhibit
- Sit down
- Lean forward—demonstrate you are interested
- Maintain open stance to show interest—implies openness and honesty when nothing is crossed (for example, arms and legs)
- Speak softly, calmly, and slowly
- Make eye contact but avoid staring—serves to build trust (you are focusing on the person and only the person)
- Avoid entering the person's personal space
- Avoid pointing at the person
- Avoid rolling your eyes
- Avoid tapping your fingers
- Avoid waiving your hands
- Avoid clenching your fists
- Avoid crossing your arms across your chest

When communicating with any difficult person establish a clear direction to where you want the discussion to go; begin with the end in mind. It is also important to focus on the pattern of communication. Be mindful if the person is not listening (wait quietly until he or she is listening), is becoming agitated and disrespectful (remain calm and reassuring), or what prompts are serving to trigger his or her hot buttons. You must be flexible in your approach to people. No two people are exactly alike. Flexibility applies to the time and setting you meet with the person as well as the flexibility in how the discussion is going. Above all else, you should be totally dedicated to finding a solution to the problem. If you are not 100-percent committed to resolving this problem you should not begin the process. Although this may be difficult, because of your mutual history, you must focus on the behavior rather than the person.

Key Preparations for Meeting with a Difficult Person

Always prepare yourself prior to meeting with a person whose behavior is difficult. You must do your homework and gather pertinent facts so that you are fully apprised of the events that have led to this problem. Listen to all parties and be objective and nonjudgmental. Do not commit yourself to a decision until you have exhausted all possibilities and have spoken to all individuals who have witnessed this conflict. Finally, you should identify priorities of this dispute so that you know what the end game should be. You can develop an action plan and share this with the effected parties. Be transparent. Always share the rationale for your decision and the mechanism you used to make your decision. This is still another way for you to build your credibility and trustworthiness in the eyes of your faculty.

No Jerks Allowed in This Department

A friend of mine, a successful businessman and former academician, who knew of my work in the area of collegiality presented

me with a book for my birthday. He indicated that there might
be "interesting corollaries" between my interest in collegiality
and the main thrust of the book. The provocatively titled book,
*The No Asshole Rule: Building a Civilized Workplace and Surviving
One That Isn't,* was written by Robert I. Sutton of Stanford University. In discussing the relevance of Sutton's book, which was
awarded a Quill Award as the best business book of 2007, to the
discussion concerning civility and conflict management, I will
substitute the third word in the title as *jerk.* Sutton indicates
that there are the following twelve (the dirty dozen) common
everyday actions that jerks use to humiliate, de-energize, or
belittle a person:

- *Personal insults.* "Wow, I can't believe you can't understand
  this." [ouch]
- *Invading one's "personal territory."* This can be represented by
  not respecting a person's office or being.
- *Uninvited physical contact.* Touching or placing hands on a
  person.
- *Threats and intimidation, both verbal and nonverbal.* "Just wait
  until you're up for tenure."
- *"Sarcastic" jokes and "teasing" used as insult-delivery systems.*
  "It's okay, Bob, after all you did graduate from an inferior
  college." [smile]
- *Withering e-mail flames.* You should always wait at least
  twenty-four hours before you respond to anyone's e-mail.
- *Status slaps intended to humiliate their victims.* "I'll speak slowly
  and only use monosyllables so even Denise can get it."
  [ouch]
- *Public shaming or "status degradation" rituals.* "Oh that's right,
  Shelley, you're only an assistant professor."
- *Rude interruptions.* Never allowing a person to complete a
  thought or sentence.

- *Two-faced attacks*. Jack tells Bill that Rick is stupid; Jack tells Rick that Bill is obese.
- *Dirty looks*. Intimidating and mean-spirited looks that can chill the blood of the victim.
- *Treating people as if they were invisible*. This is oftentimes the most unkind putdown of all. People are never listened to and are treated as if they don't exist.

The alleged jerk aims his or her venom at people who are less powerful rather than at people who are more powerful. In higher education, this is usually associated with a tenured full professor vitriolically attacking an untenured assistant professor.

Certified Jerk

We are all human beings who have subtle quirks in our personalities that manifest themselves in our behaviors. Therefore, we all have the potential to be rude and discourteous and act like jerks when we are having a bad day, when we are under pressure to complete a task, when there is a problem in our personal life, and at other times. However, the "certified jerk" is someone who *consistently* takes actions that leave a trail of victims (peers, colleagues, students, and staff) in his or her wake. This bête noire displays a persistent pattern and has a history of episodes that end with one "target" after another feeling crushed and belittled. This uncivil person makes others feel in these ways:

- Put down
- Humiliated
- Disrespected
- Oppressed
- De-energized
- Feeling worse about themselves
- Disengaged from the department and the university

It is interesting to note that 50 to 80 percent of the time nastiness and incivility is directed *by* their superiors *to* their subordinates—tenure to nontenured person. Nastiness and incivility is directed between workers of roughly the same rank from 20 to 50 percent of the time. "Upward" nastiness and incivility, whereby underdogs take on their superiors, occurs 1 percent of the time. It is also instructive to note that nastiness and incivility happens with a much greater frequency within gender— men are more likely to bully men and women to bully women. Sutton indicates that nasty interactions have a far greater impact on our moods than positive interactions, fully five times the effect.

Surfing for a Jerk

Sutton (2007) suggested that there are two tests for spotting a *jerk*:

1. After talking to the alleged [jerk], does the "target" feel oppressed, humiliated, de-energized, or belittled by the person? In particular, does the target feel worse about him- or herself?

2. Does the alleged [jerk] aim his or her venom at people who are *less powerful* rather than at those people who are *more powerful?* [p. 9]

In most places of employment being a jerk is a tremendous disadvantage. In fact, nastiness and outbursts are seen as character flaws. Their rancorous behavior makes coming to work itself an unpleasant chore. We in higher education generally have six years to make an informed decision about whether this person is one we wish to spend the next thirty years with. Chairs must be objective, honest, and fair in their evaluation of nontenured faculty—from day one up to and including their penultimate year for tenure. It is grossly unfair for a chair to continue to give a person outstanding recommendations for reappointment year after year, and then write a recommendation to not tenure that person during the year when a tenure decision is made. This is simply not fair. It is always better to be straightforward, transparent, and honest from the beginning.

Mitigating Circumstances

We all know that some people, despite their uncivil, astringent, and nasty acts, are still promoted and tenured. Are these behaviors tolerated throughout institutions of higher education where people are deemed to be more talented than the rest (for example, have $6 million in grants), are considered smarter (for example, a Nobel Award recipient or researcher of the year), are thought to be difficult to replace (teach popular courses, department depends on them for grants), and overall have a higher success rate than ordinary mortals? I have always believed that when people are classified as having "extraordinary talent" it is merely an all-purpose justification for tolerating, pampering, and kissing up to these jerks. Terms like *talented jerk, brilliant bastard*, or a *jerk and a superstar* are oxymorons. Most organizations outside of the academy strive for a "jerk free" workforce. Why should higher education be any different?

Collegiality Issues External to Institutions of Higher Education

I conducted an interview with a nonacademic in an effort to discern if there are any significant differences relative to personnel decisions between institutions of higher education and an international law firm. More specifically, I wanted to determine what role, if any, collegiality plays in advancing a lawyer's career.

Bill Swift has been involved in management of a law firm for more than twenty-seven years, including several terms as managing partner. His firm is an international law firm with offices all over the world and employs between six and seven hundred people, including more than one hundred partners. He has been a lawyer for thirty-seven years, and has been a partner in his present law firm for the past twenty-eight years. Bill is a regional senior partner. Bill (BS) and I (RC) sat down to discuss similarities between higher education and a large law firm. More specifically, the discussion focused on the importance that being collegial, respectful, and civil play in the decision to become a partner in his law firm.

RC: "Bill, thank you for agreeing to meet with me tonight. As I said to you previously, a full-time person in higher education aspires to obtain the rank of full professor and to receive tenure. Have you had occasion to deal with a non-collegial person in your law firm?"

BS: "Bob, it is a pleasure to be meeting with you. I am very interested in the topic for your book. I have seen a lack of collegiality dismantle a lawyer's career: some lawyers have the technical and commercial skills to become a partner, but because they were unpleasant and disrespectful, they were never promoted."

RC: "In our previous meetings, I explained the criteria used for tenure decisions as well as the role that collegiality may play. How does a person become a partner in your law firm?"

BS: "In order to become a partner, which is akin to attaining tenure in the academic environment, one needs to exhibit a good understanding of the law, have technical and legal skills, as well as the ability to convert that to revenue and profit for the law firm through good commercial practices (such as keeping accurate timesheets, sending out timely bills, following up with the clients, and so on). Collegiality is also a factor in that lawyers who leave a trail of destruction in their wake through bad behavior and lack of collegiality will have their progression slowed, but not necessarily ended."

RC: "Collegiality is such a difficult term to measure objectively. How do you know, with a degree of certainty, that a person is exhibiting noncollegial behavior?"

BS: "Lack of collegiality could be exhibited in constantly creating crises for subordinates and support staff, moody behavior, displays of anger, abusive language, or e-mails, and general lack of consideration for others."

RC: "How are issues of noncollegial behavior dealt with?"

BS: "All lawyers including partners are reviewed annually and if there is an issue with collegiality it will be addressed at that annual review as well as some follow-up training."

RC: "Does collegiality play a role in the decision to award a partnership?"

BS: "While collegiality certainly plays a role in the decision for advancement to partnership, it is probably the least important factor when compared to technical skills and commerciality."

RC: "This is somewhat analogous to higher education's criteria of quality teaching, scholarship (research and publications), and service as important factors in receiving tenure. Are there any other indices that you use as performance indicators for partners?"

BS: "Partners are also evaluated on their know-how, their people skills, the delivery of services, and their leadership. With regard to people skills, which are mostly closely connected to collegiality, we will look at things like acting as a leader for all employees in the firm, driving a culture of mutual respect, setting high standards, and supporting other partners to be leaders. We will also look at supervision of more junior lawyers, picking up on issues and addressing them in a sensitive and confidential manner, acting as a mentor for others, or as a sounding board on legal matters, disseminating advice on legal knowledge to less-experienced colleagues, and delivering constructive and competent feedback in all aspects of associates' work."

RC: "Okay. Suppose a person becomes a partner (that is, is tenured) and demonstrates noncollegial behavior. What, if anything, can be done to address this issue?"

BS: "If, after becoming a partner, the partner develops a lack of collegiality to the extent that the partner is becoming a detriment to the partnership as a whole, through the HR department we will seek to have the partner obtain outside training and coaching with respect to his or her behavior. This is usually done in a nonpublic way and we hope will allow the partner to see how he or she could adjust personal behavior and become more collegial."

RC: "If, however, after the interventions you describe the partner still displays this noncollegial behavior what do you do?"

BS: "It is possible that if a partner's behavior becomes so detrimental to the firm, he or she could be removed from the partnership, but this is done by a vote of the other partners and requires usually two-thirds or a 75-percent majority vote, depending on the legal partnership involved."

RC: "I want to personally thank you for sharing this information with me."

BS: "You are welcome. I enjoyed discussing this topic with you."

Communicate to Minimize Conflict

In our four-year study on department chairs (Cipriano and Riccardi, 2010; see the Appendix), the most important skill or competency that chairs reported they need was an "ability to communicate effectively."

This data-driven finding is in concert with Higgerson (1996). She wrote that "a chair's daily communication with faculty, staff, and students can do a lot to minimize destructive confrontation and set the stage for more effective conflict management when differences surface within the department" (p. 141). Higgerson (1996) indicates the following communication strategies that department chairs can follow to manage conflict.

When the chair invests in her faculty, when she is perceived as being competent, honest and fair, has good interpersonal communicative skills, is widely regarded (throughout campus and one's professional field), has well-earned credibility, is universally known to be trustworthy, and treats everyone with respect and dignity, faculty members in all likelihood will support the chair. Higgerson (1996) wrote that "if mutual respect and trust exists among colleagues, and faculty air differences openly and constructively, there is less opportunity for destructive conflicts to escalate because individuals are less prone to perceive differences of opinion as personal attacks or components of some hidden agenda" (p. 142).

Be Clear in Communicating Your Goals and Expectations for the Department and Faculty Performance

When communication is consistent and clear and when it is unmistakably understood what is valued (that is, rewarded) in the department, conflict is much less likely to occur. The chair, as the leader of the department, must make individual and department goals and expectations unambiguous and lucid to everyone. A meeting should be held in which all faculty have input regarding the goals and expectations of the department. The chair can meet individually and establish an independently prescribed set of goals with each faculty member. Of course, faculty member goals will be quite different for a junior nontenured person than they will for a tenured full professor.

Establish Ground Rules for Airing Disagreements

Conflict can be managed more effectively if there is a universally accepted and preapproved set of clearly established ground rules. Again, all faculty should be actively involved in developing the ground rules for discussing disagreements. Although there are no specific ground rules applicable for each department, Higgerson (1996) offers the following guidelines that the chair might establish:

- Abusive language will not be tolerated.

- Derogatory comments that represent personal attacks on colleagues will not be tolerated.

- Differences of opinion will be discussed and everyone will be heard.

- Department members can express their views without interruption or fear of retaliation.

- Unsubstantiated assertions will not influence the vote or outcome.

- Issues, not personalities, are subject to debate.

- Tears or emotional outbursts do not derail discussion of substantive issues.

- Department issues will be discussed and decided at department meetings, not by any subgroup of faculty. [p. 144]

Anticipate Conflict Areas and Be Ready to Intervene When Needed

An advantage of the chair walking the halls and being visible each day (rather than communicating via e-mails) is that he can anticipate potential conflicts and thus defuse them before they become full-scale problems. For example, if two graduate classes are offered one night a week, one person will teach from 5:00 to 7:30 and another person will teach from 7:35 to 10:05. A chair might anticipate that there will be a feeling or spirit of hostility and resentment from the person selected to teach the late class. A chair might defuse this situation prior to announcing the course schedule for the semester by establishing a rotation schedule whereby everyone in the department is called on to teach the late class once every five or six semesters.

Know When and How to Confront Conflict

It is vitally important that the chair manages conflict rather than become a participant in a destructive confrontation. Higgerson (1996) indicates that there are four conditions that the chair can assess to help determine when and how to confront conflict.

- *Timing.* The chair must be a manager of the conflict, not relegated to the role of a referee. When disputants are engaged in a heated argument they are exercising more emotion than logic. A chair must intervene and provide each person with an opportunity to cool down. The best way to terminate this argument is for the chair to say, "I am sure you both realize that this is embarrassing and not appropriate. Let the three of us meet and talk this through tomorrow morning at 10:00 in my office." Thus, the chair has managed the conflict by allowing the parties to cool off. The message is also clear that the problem will be addressed and not left to fester.

- *Know the facts.* We all realize that perception is not always reality. However, how a person perceives things often is reality for that person. It is important that the chair gather all the facts relative to the conflict. This entails speaking with people who witnessed the altercation. Although conflict should be managed as quickly as possible, the chair should not proceed until she has obtained all of the relevant facts.

- *Depersonalize the issue.* It is important that the chair not allow the personalities and past history of the disputants to blur the facts. It is difficult to be totally objective when a person is yelling and being disrespectful to you. It is also not easy to be free of bias when you know the disputants well and have worked closely with each of them for a number of years. As hard as it may be, the chair must focus with laserlike intensity on the issue(s) rather than the personalities of the people involved. A chair is the leader of the department and must act like one. This includes consistent behavior and demeanor toward every faculty member in the department and not allowing the appearance of favoritism to creep into any discussions regarding the performance of faculty members as well as the chair.

- *Don't prolong the confrontation.* Chairs must have a short memory and not carry a grudge; they simply cannot afford to perseverate on the past if they expect faculty members to carry their weight in the overall efficiency of the department. How the chair responds after a dispute is managed and settled can go a long way in current and future relationships with members of the faculty. Normal communication should be restored quickly, which will place the past disagreement in a bigger, more useful context.

Know When and How to Initiate Conflict

Those disagreements that are not dealt with have the potential to become insidious and dangerous to the morale of the department. The chair should initiate conflict and allow the disagreement to be aired in a constructive and positive way. An example is illustrative of this point. Jim, an untenured assistant professor in my department, was selected to present a keynote address at a national conference. I held a department meeting in which I indicated that our department budget would support Jim in going to the conference in view of the fact that (1) it was a keynote address, (2) it would bring recognition to the department, and (3) this would help his promotion and tenure efforts. All faculty members were in agreement that this was a good decision for Jim and the department. I wanted each faculty member to have an opportunity to express his or her thoughts in an open meeting. This transparency was appreciated and served as a consistent leadership technique throughout my term as chair.

Recognize Which Conflicts Are Yours to Manage

The salient question for determining if a conflict is the chair's to manage is, "Does the conflict affect the overall productivity or morale of the department?" If the answer is yes, the chair has a responsibility to manage the conflict. If the answer is no, the chair should be grateful and move on to other department responsibilities.

"Academic environments that successfully manage conflict through valuing openness, civility, and honest communication are more likely to survive."

—E. Creamer (2004)

Turning a Conflict into a Problem to Be Managed

Academics pride themselves in their ability to problem solve. Our academic education and training, as manifested by writing our dissertations and developing research protocols, consists of selecting a problem and finding solutions to the problem. Cheldelin and Lucas (2004) wrote that "nonjudgmental listening . . . is the single most important tool in handling conflict effectively" (p. 47).

Ways to Manage Conflict

I have found that when I adhere to the following, I am able to more readily manage conflict:

- *Communicate!* Open communication lines are needed. Engagement and good communication are keys in managing conflict.
- *Establish ground rules for airing disagreements.* This works much better if buy-in by all faculty members has occurred prior to a disagreement.
- *Listen.* Listening is a skill whose importance cannot be overstated. Paraphrasing what you hear the other person

saying shows the person that you are trying to comprehend his point of view.

- *Monitor and control your emotions.* As previously stated, inappropriate expressions of anger serves no useful purpose. Emotional responses uttered in the heat of an argument can damage relationships for years to come.
- *Set the stage.* You must set the time and place for a meeting between the disputants, gather all of the facts, and have a result that you would like to see come out of this meeting.
- *Understand exactly what the dispute is about.* Avoid making assumptions.
- *Always address the issue.* Not addressing the issue in the hope that it will go away heightens the tension and increases collateral damage.
- *Engage.* Engagement leads to managing problems and preserving relationships.
- *Always do your homework.* Need to frame, fact-find, and reframe.
- *Try to handle issues informally whenever possible.* Issues that are handled formally can present many present and future relationship problems.

What Is Not Pleasant but Absolutely Needed?

Department chairs, like the majority of people, do not like to manage conflict. However, it is an essential part of the role and responsibility of chairs. Apparently, managing conflict is becoming more of a need in higher education. It is very important that department chairs develop a good support system. Chairs should seek out colleagues in the university to talk to and get good advice.

Problem

You are the chair of a department of seven full-time faculty members. One of your faculty colleagues, Dr. Crotchety, is a tenured full professor who has been at the university for thirty-one years. You have had a somewhat frosty and inconsistent relationship with him over the past six years of your chairpersonship. He displays a pleasant demeanor when things go his way. However, he becomes nasty when he doesn't get his way. In the past, Dr. Crotchety always was scheduled to teach his classes on Tuesdays and Thursdays. This semester, however, you had to change his teaching schedule to include Mondays, Wednesdays, and Fridays. He e-mails you a terse message indicating he wants to see you in your office tomorrow morning at 10:00 to discuss his teaching schedule. You fully anticipate an unpleasant meeting. At precisely 10:00 he storms into your office and commences yelling at you indicating that you had no right to change his schedule. He is becoming more and more belligerent in both his verbal and nonverbal communication. He is screaming at you in a bellicose manner. You realize that you must "do something" to quell this angry argument. So, what do you do?

Possible Solution

Communicating with an angry person should not be a competition to see "who wins." Being a good and experienced communicator, you shift the exchange from the highly emotional to the rational. Empathize with Dr. Crotchety. Change "I" to "you": "*I* appreciate *your* frustration." "*I* understand *your* doubt." "*I* share *your* concern." Also, use the "I, too" phrase that lets Dr. Crotchety know that you, too, feel or have felt in the past the same way. "I also felt the way you do now." "I, too, have felt that way." "I, too, would want to know the same thing if I were in your position." Your objective of this method of communicating is to let

Dr. Crotchety calm down. Further, you could request his permission to ask the following: "Would it be helpful for you to know what we have done in this area thus far?" "What information can I provide you?" "Would it be helpful to you if we . . . ?"

CASE STUDY

Conclusion

We know that there are both positive and negative effects of conflict. We also know that conflict is inevitable. The chair is placed in the rather unenviable position of being the person who must manage this conflict in order for her department to function successfully. An effective chair is also an effective communicator. It is important for the chair to recognize how and when to turn a conflict into a problem to be managed. That the chair has an important role to play in managing conflict is accurate. However, it is also important that the university as a whole does not abrogate its responsibilities in this area.

Chapter Five provides the reader with specific insights into how the university as a whole can supply the necessary resources and support needed to facilitate a collegial and civil campus.

5

UNIVERSITY-WIDE RESPONSIBILITIES IN PROMOTING A COLLEGIAL CAMPUS

Dumbo the elephant believed that what allowed
him to fly was the feather the crows had given him.
Only when he drops the feather does he realize that
he truly has the gift of flight.

I continue to be somewhat mystified that the department chair is perceived as *the* person responsible for managing the behavior of an uncivil, noncollegial, and nasty person in the department. Logically, because of the following (not a complete) list, a chair may not be the best person to have to deal with a toxic faculty member by themselves. Chairs

First and foremost are faculty members and consider
themselves as such

Are sometimes (most of the time?) elected by full-time
members of the department

Serve for as little as three years; the average length of time to
serve as chair is six years

Return as a faculty member within their department when
their tenure as chair ends

Have not had any training or education in working with an
abusive, toxic, and mean faculty member

Interact regularly (daily?) with faculty members in the
department

Need faculty members to volunteer to serve on a variety of department, school and university-wide committees

Try to gain consensus to move the department's agenda

Would like all faculty members to share in the department's work load equitably

Indicate that the most important reasons they leave the chair position are

- Lack of authority commensurate with their responsibilities
- Lack of control associated with their daily bureaucratic grind of mind-numbing paperwork
- Lack of time for their own creative work
- Inability to manage destructive conflict within the department

Indicate that the five most important skills, in order of priority, that they need to fulfill their responsibilities as chair are

- Ability to communicate effectively
- Interpersonal skills
- Character and integrity
- Leadership skills
- Problem-solving ability

Perhaps the very nature of the duties of a department chair can serve as fuel to ignite incivility by a faculty member toward the chair. Conceivably, it could be that the person that has borne the most responsibility in managing an uncivil faculty member may be the person that is placed in this unenviable position *because* of the nature of the job—the department chair. The chair is regularly called on to make decisions, which may lead to anger, frustration, and hostility toward the chair by faculty members.

- *Assign courses to faculty members.* This may cause conflicts wherein a faculty member may want to teach one course but it is given to another to teach.

- *Offer summer contracts.* Oftentimes faculty members want to work during the summer months in order to obtain additional pay as well as to have a larger payout for their retirement.
- *Assign days and times for faculty members to teach.* Faculty members may want a two-day-a-week teaching schedule, may not want to teach during the evening or on the weekend, or may only want morning classes.
- *Recommend salary increases.* This is usually associated with merit raises. Although the money is not significant, the ego is!
- *Recommend personnel decisions.* The chair is responsible for recommending faculty for reappointment, promotion in rank, sixth-year posttenure review, and tenure. In some institutions of higher learning, chairs also can recommend that a special assessment be conducted relative to a faculty member's performance.
- *Assign office space.* Larger offices and offices with windows are precious commodities that may sow seeds for conflict. Do the faculty members with the longest tenure in the university get the nicest offices? Do the most productive faculty? Is the determination by rank? Does the chair establish a lottery method for assigning offices?
- *Assign graduate assistants.* Faculty members usually clamor for a graduate assistant to help in myriad ways. Do chairs assign graduate assistants to faculty on a rotating basis? Strictly on faculty research productivity? A lottery method?
- *Fill open and needed positions in the department.* When an opportunity to hire a new faculty member presents itself, which qualifications are the most important for the department to move forward on? This can cause rancor between the "specialists" in the department who are all advocating for their area of expertise or specialization.

- *Stipulate the use of student workers.* What criteria the chair establishes to assign student workers to faculty is important in its perception of fairness as well as what is in the best interest of the department.

- *Specify use of and work of secretaries.* The chair oftentimes prioritizes in what order the secretary performs his work.

- *Determine access to computers—home and on campus.* Chairs often make the decision concerning which faculty members are able to have a computer to use at home.

- *Award travel support.* Faculty members want to travel to conferences and workshops to make presentations or attend sessions. The department budget is managed by the chair. Therefore, the responsibility of determining who receives the financial resources to attend conferences is made by the chair.

- *Determine committee assignments.* Faculty members are expected to serve on department, school, and university-wide committees. Some committees require greater time commitments than others.

- *Determine budget needs of the department or faculty.* The disposition of the department budget can energize people to strike out against the person allocating these resources—the department chair.

- *Intervene in student-generated complaints against faculty member.* The chair is professionally obligated to follow through with any and all complaints filed by students against a faculty member.

- *Observe faculty members teaching.* A classroom is considered sacrosanct to most faculty members. Also, faculty members do not believe that a chair knows anything more about quality instruction than they do.

- *Determine efficacy of research.* Chairs are not selected because of their demonstrated expertise in research. Yet, chairs are required to make judgments regarding a faculty member's research for personnel decisions.

- *Evaluate the effectiveness of advising students.* This is, at best, an inexact science. Therefore, a less-than-stellar evaluation leaves the door open for conflict.
- *Assess the value of the faculty member's service to the department, the school, the university, and the community.* "Service" can be interpreted by many different people in many different ways.

The decisions that chairs make on an everyday basis can cause explosive reactions by faculty members who may envision that the chair has a personal vendetta against them. The counter-measure to this thinking is when the chair establishes a history of being honest, competent, fair, trustworthy, credible, and treats all people with respect and dignity. When a chair displays these character traits in a consistent way, faculty members are much more likely to give a chair the benefit of the doubt.

Question: "What can or should a dean do to help a depart-ment chair deal with an uncivil faculty member?"

*   *   *

Answer: "A dean has to be the 'guide on the side' to help department chairs deal with uncivil faculty—coaching, sup-porting, and assisting department chairs. This can start with basic training and development of department chairs in 'principled' conflict resolution to direct intervention if needed by the chair and department. At one university, the dean even removed a faculty member from all department meet-ings and had the faculty member report directly to the dean."
—Walter H. Gmelch, dean, School of Education, University of San Francisco

(*continued*)

(*continued*)

Answer: "Support and be sure he or she is documenting each incident. Thanks to your work, I'm also able to cite a lawsuit that supports dismissal based on lack of collegiality."
—Susan Hannam, dean, College of Health, Environment and Science, Slippery Rock University

Answer: "The dean has the authority to suggest counseling, constant monitoring, or a letter in personnel file that could lead to termination." —Roger L. Coles, interim dean, Graduate Studies, Central Michigan University

Changing Dynamics of Higher Education

The landscape of higher education for the sixteen hundred public and two thousand private institutions of higher education is rapidly changing and constantly evolving (ostensibly on a daily basis). The past few years has seen a dichotomy in many aspects of higher education. Note some of the contradictions:

- American higher education remains the envy of the world. Seventeen of the twenty top-rated universities in the world are in the United States. Also, thirty-six of the top fifty rated universities in the world are in the United States (Goldin, 2010). However, our graduation rates are woefully low: a pitiable 55 percent of students graduate from college within six years. Fewer than 30 percent of full-time students who begin at a community college graduate with an associate degree in three years. In addition, 35 percent of college students are taking at least one year of remedial coursework.
- the cost of a college education has grown much faster than costs of other goods and services. In 2008, five colleges charged at least $50,000 a year for tuition, fees, room, and board. In 2009, fifty-eight colleges charged at least $50,000 a

year for tuition, fees, room, and board. Patrick Callan, president of the National Center for Public Policy and Higher Education, found that college tuition and fees increased 439 percent from 1982 to 2007, while median family income rose 147 percent. "If we go this way for another twenty-five years, we won't have an affordable system of higher education" (Callan, 2008, p. A19).

- The gap between median annual earnings of people with bachelor's degrees and those with high school degrees but no college is $19,911. Twelve percent of mail carriers have college degrees. In 1986, the average federal, need-based Pell grant covered 98 percent of tuition at a public four-year school, where 70 percent of American students attend (more than twelve million students). Today, these grants cover only 53 percent of tuition.

- After World War II, the United States was the undoubted world leader in higher education. But past success bred complacency. Other developed nations now produce more college graduates per capita and China and India, because of their sheer size, turn out graduates in greater numbers. Out of every one hundred American ninth-graders, only forty will enter college right out of high school, and just eighteen of those will graduate by their twenty-fifth birthday.

From 1945 to 1975, student enrollment in institutions of higher education increased 500 percent to eleven million students. There were many external reasons for this unprecedented increase: the GI Bill, the unpopular war in Vietnam and the attendant risk of being drafted, Sputnik was sent into orbit by the Soviet Union, a population explosion, a rise in the belief of the value of a college education, and so on. In response to this rise in the number of students attending institutions of higher education, and those who wanted to attend but could not, greater resources were provided to the nation's colleges and universities. Campus-building programs were begun, colleges and universities hired more faculty members and staff to help meet the expanding student population, and the government provided financial incentives in the form of grants and scholarships so as to make the cost of a college education financially viable. The states also picked up their fair share to facilitate the growth of colleges and universities through state budget allocations earmarked for higher education. Collectively, states still spend about $70 billion per year on higher education but its share of overall spending has dropped dramatically. Higher education made up more than 15 percent of state budgets a generation ago; today the number is more like 10 percent (Greenblatt, 2007). Greenblatt (2007) wrote that "as recently as 1980, states supplied about half of the revenues at public colleges and universities, but now state funds account for less than one-third." Also, the erratic manner in which state funding is allocated militates against long-term planning: states are generous in good times but stingy during recessions.

From 2000 to 2006, college enrollment rose 17 percent. The number of people attending both two- and four-year colleges and universities in the United States reached 20.5 million in 2006, an increase of 3 million students since 2000. There are now 17.1 million undergraduate and 3.4 million graduate students in graduate or professional schools. Undergraduate enrollment grew from 14.4 million in 2000 to 17.1 million in 2006. The University of Phoenix has a mind-numbing 443,000 students! It also has a 16-percent six-year graduation rate and 95 percent of its faculty members are part-time.

Paradoxically, while enrollment is at an all-time high, our colleges and universities are beset with myriad challenges:

- Tenure is being attacked both externally and within the academy.
- Forty percent of the 595,000 full-time professors are over the age of fifty-five.
- The state of the economy ("My 401 is now a 201!") has militated against many professors retiring.

- Retirement benefits and fringe benefits are being eroded.
- Tenure and tenure-track positions are dwindling at an alarming rate.
- Budgets of all institutions of higher education are being cut dramatically.
- Furlough days are becoming the norm, along with no pay raises for faculty members and staff.
- Professors are being expected to teach more, and larger class size is the new standard.
- The hiring of adjuncts has militated against the hiring of more full-time professors.
- There is pressure to accept more students, including those who may not be ready to attend an institution of higher education as a full-time student.
- There is an apparent dearth of full-time faculty, tenure-track positions.

These challenges have taken place within a relatively brief time period. Most institutions of higher education are not prepared to move quickly and proactively to meet these challenges head on. It is true that institutions of higher education move in a ponderous manner. Some might even suggest that this is due to the bureaucratic nature of institutions of higher education. The saliency of this point is given as a note of caution when strategies are presented regarding how institutions of higher education can implement policies to facilitate a more collegial campus.

Question: "What supports, if any, should institutions of higher education provide to help a department chair deal with an uncivil, noncollegial faculty member?"

*   *   *

(continued)

(*continued*)

Answer: "Administrative support and education of the faculty union (if unionized) so that its members understand and embrace the importance of civility." —Susan Hannam, dean, College of Health, Environment and Science, Slippery Rock University

Question: "What can happen if incivility takes over a department?"

*   *   *

Answer: "The lack of civility can *kill* a department. I can think of two examples, one where the department was eliminated at a large Research 1 East Coast university and in another large midwestern university the chair stepped down because of the infighting. In this particular department two faculty members who literally sat back to back to each other in the same office suite refused to verbally communicate with each other and used only e-mails to correspond to each other." —Roger L. Coles, interim dean, Graduate Studies, Central Michigan University

Answer: "A university should provide initial training with professional consultants as part of the initial orientation when a chairperson is selected. This should include workshops on how to accept and respond to concerns. Additional workshops for interviewing, recommending change of behavior, university policies, and university support programs should be provided." —Bruce W. Russell, dean, College of Business, Information, and Social Sciences, Slippery Rock University

Answer: "Competent human resource departments might provide assistance with such interventions. At one university, the department of counseling and psychology also volunteered assistance to other departments needing help."

—Walter H. Gmelch, dean, School of Education, University of San Francisco

Answer: "The primary support that we can provide is to work to help change the faculty member's behavior. In the case of a newer faculty member—that is, untenured—we would most likely not renew. However, once a faculty member is tenured and promoted, we have few carrots left and must rely on helping the faculty member get better (through counseling or whatever) or we can start requiring the faculty member to undergo interim reviews to address the problems. Usually when we start down this road, the condition ends in legal action." —William R. Williams, provost and vice president for academic affairs, Slippery Rock University

Answer: "On-campus resources (counseling department, law school, human resources, and so on) should be made available to chairs to offer guidance, support, and when necessary, service. Also the university should make sure that human resources policies, procedures, and practices are current and reflect the universities agenda of creating and sustaining a collegial, civil environment." —Jim MacGregor, chair, Department of Recreation and Leisure Studies, Southern Connecticut State University.

University-Wide Responsibilities for Fostering Collegiality

There should be an expectation that collegiality, respect, and civility will permeate the climate of the college or university. Just as the chair is the key player in setting the tone, climate, and culture within her department, there are many resources that the college or university can call on to establish a climate that values civility, by its words and its actions, that sends a clear and unambiguous message regarding the importance of collegiality. The actions may include terminating a person whose behavior continues to constitute incivility and a clear disrespect for his colleagues. Buller (2010) indicated that even tenured faculty members may be reprimanded or dismissed for a lack of collegiality. He does make a strong statement that events must be thoroughly documented:

> Particularly in cases where an employee is being dismissed, whatever form of due process the institution provides will inevitably offer the employee an opportunity to dispute or reply to any supervisor's claim of unsatisfactory performance. It's in the institution's best interests, therefore, to have documented cases of problems that were caused or opportunities that were lost because of how the employee acted rather than insubstantial claims of a widespread perception of other such impressions that can't be tied to explicit behavior. [p. 3]

Chairs should not be left to single-handedly deal with an uncivil, disrespectful, and noncollegial faculty member. A department chair should be viewed as one of many university constituencies that work collaboratively to rein in an uncivil person. The most effective approach is one that addresses the concerns of incivility, non-collegiality and lack of respect in a systematic manner. There should be university-wide policies established that promote collegiality, civility, and respect campuswide. Universally applied reward and reprimand systems should be established and consistently followed. It is true that what gets rewarded gets repeated. Therefore, noncollegial behavior must be addressed as quickly as possible. You do not want to send the wrong meaning that noncollegial behavior will be "smiled away" in the hope that it will not reoccur. The erroneous message can be delivered whereby if a person yells and is nasty she will get what she wants. That is rewarding a negative behavior—which will repeat itself and be manifested in other ways. It is important that all safeguards concerning academic freedom and shared governance be in place prior to initiating any policy. All segments of the university community must have open dialogues before applying the following recommendations and strategies for fostering collegiality (Gappa, Austin, and Trice, 2007):

- "Encourage faculty members to take personal responsibility for the quality of their academic community and the professional behavior of their colleagues." [p. 309]
- "Find ways to include all faculty members in explicit and welcoming ways to the institution's community." [p. 310]
- "Provide gathering spaces and meeting rooms at a variety of campus locations to bring faculty members together outside of their academic departments for informal interactions." [p. 315]
- "Provide structured opportunities for faculty members to interact with colleagues around topics of intellectual interest." [p. 315]

Universities can implement the following strategies to facilitate a more civil, collegial, and respectful campus:

Include the expectation of civility, respect, and collegiality in the university's mission statement.

Educate and train members of the faculty senate and department evaluation committee on the importance of collegiality.

Publicize the values of a collegial relationship through human resources and the equity and diversity offices.

Provide professional development workshops to all faculty members on the topic of collegiality.

Prominently feature the importance of civility and respect in position announcements for new faculty.

Encourage search committees to specify collegiality in interview questions.

Conduct campuswide dialogues on civility and collegiality.

Clearly state expectations for civil behavior for faculty, staff, students, and the administration in the faculty handbook.

Adopt a workplace harassment policy that encompasses more than just sexual harassment.

Implement and consistently reinforce clearly stated sanctions—up to and including termination.

Educate and train members of the campuswide tenure and promotion committee on the importance of collegiality.

Indicate in the collective bargaining agreement, if applicable, that a proper academic climate can be maintained only when faculty members display civility and collegiality.

Educate chairs and deans in conflict management, resolving conflict, and pre- and postconflict communication techniques.

Establish universal ground rules for airing disagreements.

Facilitate campuswide workshops about the importance of the university climate on morale and productivity.

Launch a training program to educate chairs and deans in knowing when and how to confront departmental conflict.

Develop a university-wide code of ethics that is endorsed by faculty members, staff, and administrators.

Create a campus culture that encourages faculty members to hold each other accountable for professional standards of behavior.

Enact a campuswide goal of including all faculty members in welcoming ways.

Facilitate interdisciplinary learning communities to enhance collaboration.

Build a supporting coalition of informal and formal peacemakers.

Gather documented support from the faculty senate, president, provost, deans, chairs, and faculty that noncollegial behavior will not be tolerated.

Develop a series of training sessions to educate the campus community on documenting what constitutes a lack of civility, respect, and collegiality.

Make collegiality the fourth criteria for tenure along with teaching, scholarship, and service.

Give chairs the authority to recommend that a special assessment be conducted on a noncollegial faculty member:

- Strictly adhere to specific protocols and safeguards.

- Identify problem(s) with a faculty member's performance and, if needed, develop a plan of improvement to address these specific problems.

- Have the dean and chair meet to design appropriate evaluations and assessments of the faculty member.

- Assign experienced and trained evaluator(s) to work with the faculty member to become a more valued and valuable member of the university community.

- Have evaluator(s) develop specific intervention strategies to help the faculty member.

- Have evaluator(s) submit a written report to the dean, chair, and affected faculty member with recommended actions.

- Implement and evaluate a specific plan with a detailed schedule of compliance.

Faculty input is essential when formulating principles and policies based on any of these strategies. Full and thoughtful deliberations will serve, at the very least, to bring the importance of collegiality to the forefront of a variety of constituencies throughout the university community. It is also important that adequate resources are forthcoming from the central administration in designing the plan as well as implementing and evaluating its effi-cacy. "A college or university's efforts to achieve a collegial com-munity is a crucial and lasting investment in its most precious resource: its faculty members and the intellectual capital they bring to their campus and their work" (Gappa, Austin, and Trice, 2010, p. 320).

CASE STUDY

Problem

You are a new chair who was hired from another university; therefore, you have little or no knowledge of where the power lies within your new university. You currently have a unified staff of nine full-time faculty members in your de-partment. All of the faculty members are tenured and each has been at the university for a minimum of eight years to a maximum of twenty-one years. At your previous university you saw firsthand how important it was to identify the key stakeholders. These people were able to aid in bringing many of the goals of the department to fruition. You realize that you will need to quickly establish a good working relationship with key people to facilitate the growth and well-being of your department. How will you go about build-ing bridges to establish a good working affiliation with some key individuals?

Possible Solutions

- Hold a department meeting and establish unanimity of the importance of building bridges with a key person within the university.
- Identify a person (for example, a dean) whom your department needs to develop a successful relationship with to be successful.
- Establish the specific types of help you need.
- Establish specific input that this person needs from your department.

- Identify common objectives you share with this person or stakeholder.
- Brainstorm any barriers that may prevent this person and your department from working together.
- Agree on what member of your department would be the best person to be the main contact with this person.
- Determine what steps your department can take to develop a positive relationship and obtain the necessary assistance from this stakeholder.

Conclusion

Collegiality and civility should be viewed as a university-wide phenomenon. All of the considerable resources of the university should be called on to promote and facilitate a collegial campus. University administrations must do their part to empower chairs with the means to lead a nontoxic department. Faculty members also should speak out against the vitriolic antics of their peers who are causing much discord.

Chapter Six provides the reader with examples of correct alignment that can be used to promote the core academic mission of the university. Collegiality is looked at through the prism of chairs, deans, and chief academic officers. The chapter also presents a section on cyberbullying about which the great majority of chairs will be able to relate.

6

STRUCTURAL REALIGNMENT, BUDGETARY SUPPORT, AND CYBERBULLYING

Ellen R. Beatty

Pity for the guilty is treason to the innocent.
—*Ayn Rand (1975)*

Historically, the chief academic officer was the first among equals in steering the academic enterprise within the university. In institutions of higher education, traditionally, the president relied on the academic vice president (AVP) to be the academic leader of the institution. This may no longer be necessarily true in emerging organizational structures within modern universities. The role of the chief financial officer has taken on increasing prominence in the modern college and university. It may now be quite common to have vice presidents of finance, development, and human resources thereby elevating these positions to equal footing at the administrative cabinet level. To counter this emerging phenomenon some institutions have developed the AVP role into a combination provost position in an attempt to realign the importance of academic responsibilities within the institution.

As welcome and perhaps necessary and vital as these evolving roles are, they have the risk of eroding the influence of the academic core mission. This is an example of misalignment in structure that may cause considerable, although unintended, harm to the academy. This book discusses the facilitation of collegiality. This chapter examines the exciting possibility of a new alignment, one that incorporates the chairperson as the link between the faculty and the administration directed toward creating a true collegial environment. Fogg (2003) stated that the hierarchy is a natural incubator of conflict. So why not change the structure to bring about better outcomes in terms of collegiality?

Structural Misalignment That May Damage Collegiality

Another example illustrates how changing roles need careful attention in our discussion of collegiality. It is now common for directors of institutional development and human resources to be elevated to vice presidential levels (due to importance of equity issues and questions of institutional liability) to serve in the administrative cabinet. These individuals may have the same voice and vote as the chief academic officer with their own budgets and responsibilities that do not necessarily align with the academic vision and goals for the institution. This might be justifiable if "new" monies were available but the base budgets for institutions are decreasing rather than increasing. Without any new monies or resources to the university, the chief information officer (CIO) may have an independent budget with responsibilities to infuse technology into the teaching and learning process. This initiative, although representing a welcome advance in academia, might be more correctly placed within the province of the chief academic officer or as a shared responsibility.

A Vision Defeated by Misalignment of Role with Negative Impact on Collegiality

In a third example, the Department of Recreation and Leisure Studies embarked on an initiative to develop a center for nonprofit organizations. This represented a compelling vision for the future of the program and had strong stakeholder support from community organizations. Most of the agencies expressing interest had been involved with student internships and were familiar with the academic program. Nonprofit agencies face unusual fiscal constraints and welcomed a center that offered the promise of advocacy, research, and support for the common goals of all nonprofit organizations. This nonprofit initiative might have launched a transformation of the delivery of the curriculum within the program. The goals were to engage faculty to focus on student learning, student participation, and student research. The project was derailed due to a misalignment of staff and structure. The vice president for institutional development, who held an equal place as the AVP on the university cabinet, objected to the establishment of a center for nonprofits. The argument was made that such partnerships with community agencies at the academic program level would threaten future fundraising efforts. This does not make sense because effective community partnerships through high level student and faculty engagement serve only to heighten the opinion of community stakeholders. Such activities often result in the real perception that the institution is giving back to the community in important ways. This story represents a lost opportunity to collaborate with the community while restructuring educational delivery to focus on student outcomes. Ironically, there was a lost potential revenue stream regarding future grant-writing opportunities. One can not discount the high cost in faculty cynicism as decisions about the academic enterprise are seen as beholden to other than academic professionals within the university. This was clearly the chairperson's call with support from the chief academic officer. Misalignment of staffing roles and responsibilities gave way to a critical strategic misstep.

What Might Have Happened Instead

A small nonprofit agency that had student interns requested that a community-needs assessment be undertaken. The agency was interested in developing a new program but simply did not have the staffing capacity or human power skill set to perform the necessary preliminary research. Under the supervision of a faculty member, the students did the following:

- Conducted the needs assessment
- Assisted the agency significantly
- Learned much about the local community
- Developed preprofessional skills necessary for their selected major
- Enjoyed the work immensely
- Collaborated with colleagues in the agency and field
- Served as effective ambassadors for the university
- Actually created a measurable learning outcome: the needs assessment

This chair changed the focus from how much the faculty member teaches to the nature of what and how much the student learns. Rather than take a course in the nature of nonprofit organizations, the student would have the real opportunity to work with faculty guidance. The problem became one of credit allocation for the faculty member. This was an alternative route to the usual class lecture model that is often used successfully in independent study projects and in graduate education. This proved problematic at the undergraduate level simply because there was no easy applicable model to use. The curriculum was designed traditionally along seat time, classroom hours, and grades rather than learning outcomes. Curricular redesign takes effort and time but also allows the program to be nimble in responding to educational opportunities in the community such as this one.

Correct Alignment That Promotes the Academic Core Mission

A good example related to technology illustrates the correct alignment of structure and role. After a few years of collaborating with deans about faculty development, we were successful at generating active participation among the faculty in better utilization of technology to improve teaching and learning processes. As vice president in the academic world of meager resources, I was able to obtain ample if not substantial funding to establish competitive internal grants and support for the innovative pedagogical use of technology. Much important groundwork had been undertaken and academic affairs had the attention and eager participation of the faculty. Modest incentives of time, money, and information technology (IT) support resources served as powerful incentives. Faculty members and many chairpersons gathered together during noncontract time periods for a summer technology workshop geared to support their early work with pedagogy and technology. The project was an outstanding success with requests for "Winter Tech" and "Spring Tech." Radiating from the faculty surveys were requests for more, more, more! Remember, early on when pundits predicted incorrectly that the faculty would not embrace technology? As a result of this project, along with the development of requisite technological skills, the creation of a true community of scholars interested primarily in good teaching and in technology for improvement of student learning emerged.

Misalignment That Places
the Academic Mission at Risk

Contrast this previous positive example with the more likely misalignment in structure and roles that occurs within many colleges and universities. The IT unit grows quickly and insidiously without the proper planning of key academic players (for example, chairs) to maximize the impact on student-centered learning. Often this can occur in tandem with large expenditures of budgetary resources. Colleges can distribute the resources to IT personnel who then work individually with faculty without a sense of the overall plan for the infusion of technology into the learning process. My previous example of a successful technology workshop project based on a modest budget item had a much stronger collective effect of creating a community of faculty scholars identified and committed to the effective and creative use of technology to support pedagogy. This project surely demonstrates the momentum toward becoming a community of scholars that is so essential for a collegial organization.

I am emphasizing budget in this discussion of collegiality. It is not necessarily the amount, *but the capacity to influence budget that will give the chair the powerful tool and efficacy to build community*. Small rewards such as internal research grants, curricular grants, and reassigned time can be tied to participation in the community. There simply must be rewards and punishments (disincentives), a cost to being noncollegial when so much is at stake for higher education.

Consequences of Not Choosing Collegiality as the Guiding Principle and Outcome

Fast forward eight years later in this same university when the budget for IT had mushroomed while the academic affairs budget specific to technology had diminished. Actually, the amount of base funding was similar but allocated to the IT unit rather than to academic affairs, a strategic budgetary misalignment for sure. Representing a chairperson of a department, I approached the CIO to request training to incorporate social networking. My intention was to free up a small amount of funding to incorporate social networking software (Twitter, Facebook, and so on) into the curriculum. The resources to assist faculty to enhance these emerging technologies to support curriculum in alignment with current student use should have come from resources available within the academic budget, not the other way around. This chair was left with the sole option of applying to the IT services unit with a proposal to obtain funding for an important academic project. The chair representing the faculty can communicate student needs better than anyone else because he or she is at the point of service. The AVP, in accord with the vision of the department, must be able to access funds on behalf of the chair who represents faculty members, students, and programmatic needs.

The chief academic officer can support the chair to bring faculty members along in accord with stated department goals. Information technology personnel should not be authorized to decide what is best for the academic unit. Even with good intentions, scarce resources should not be used to advance individual faculty goals and aspirations concerning technology. A university-wide plan should guide such expenditures of human and budgetary resources for the benefit of academic programming.

Misalignment of Results Due to Misplaced and Inauthentic Collegiality

This same principle of proper alignment can be used to carefully evaluate other areas of new expenditure. It becomes quite useful to hold the action (for example, funding any endeavor) up to scrutiny. If the institution has a strategic plan to internationalize the campus, the budget must be carefully tendered. One vice president of development selected a few study abroad programs that were appealing and interesting. Certain students, but not all, were then able to access funds for these study abroad programs. Should this be the method of deciding who obtains discretionary funding? Should nonacademic areas such as institutional development have funding for strategic initiatives that affect academic programs so obviously? Faculty members eagerly accepted the financial assistance that was arbitrarily offered. Should not the faculty be wiser than to accept funding so clearly misaligned? The funding was legitimate; this was never the question or the issue. But the actions, however well intentioned, interfered with program delivery at the department level and skirted the chair. Such actions may have satisfied a few individual faculty members but caused the usual generic problems of misplaced authority. Most important, this story illustrates the results of a lack of collegiality:

- Failure to document need, which is the first principle of policy change
- Did not advance the development of internationalization on campus
- No accountability; even the chair did not know how many students or how much funding was allocated
- Haphazard and out-of-alignment results; without establishing criteria some programs were funded but not others
- Peerage system of granting favor to those influential faculty members (for example, senate and union leaders) who may reciprocate by supporting administrative agendas or platforms
- Side-stepped strategic plans of departments, chairs, deans, and the chief academic officer

In research parlance, this might be considered a "type two error," failure to reject the null hypothesis. Only novice AVPs and chairs should make such mistakes. It is very necessary with effective leadership to create the sense of community so essential for true collegiality. The departmental chair is part of a greater and larger community of the university that will thrive best if all individual pieces are aligned and in competition with one another. Budgets must always be considered as part of a coordinated effort and plan (Wergin, 2003).

Faculty Members Suspicious of Success in Other Units of the System

The considerable efforts to move us forward as a regional graduate center were jeopardized permanently by a few who supported only initiatives deemed helpful to the general education curriculum. This was myopic at best and could have been mitigated through a partnership with chairs who are perfectly capable of looking beyond self-interest.

At the university level, there is need for budgetary allocations to support both thriving professional schools and the undergraduate college mission. Individual faculty members can learn to be self-serving because this has been the name of the game in academe for so long. Often individuals must advocate and compete for limited resources in a strident effort to obtain money for initiatives. How can one expect the faculty members to operate any other way if this has been the modus operandi for so long? Chairs carefully included in open and authentic assessment of budgetary problems and solutions can become important partners in such critical endeavors. If this individual faculty member had been patient, a natural alignment would have occurred; additional revenue allocated by formula for graduate education would have added to the overall budget of the institution to use for all undergraduate programs. Instead, this faculty leader led the cry for the campus to become the state leader in liberal education. Sounds reasonable, except it was in contradiction to a publicly articulated invitation from the chancellor to become a leading center for graduate study in the region. This is comparable to a high school with a championship lacrosse team. When the success of the one athletic program is featured in the press, and to important stakeholders in the community, would others in the school object? Would genuine success of one component of the athletic program be viewed as diminishing to other athletic programs? Would students and coaches declare publicly that their basketball team is just as good but just hadn't had the same opportunity to excel as the lacrosse team? Of course not! This is an example of lost opportunity and misalignment of values. With a better use of the chair in a true collegial partnership with deans, the AVP and other administrators would have mediated such a scenario. There should not have been a "we versus them," "graduate versus undergraduate" competition. This was a call for true collegiality defined in the simplest sense as the noun: *cooperative action among colleagues*. This would have yielded a better outcome in the long term.

Chair Role Is Ambiguous but It Can Be a Guiding Light to Advance the Mission of the Department

Chairs can be taken into confidence by deans, the AVP, and provost and become privy to information that they are capable of comprehending due to unique and varied experiences at the program level with faculty, students, and the community. The AVP and provost must capitalize on this rich human resource of chairs to augment the efforts of deans. There need not be fear of breaks in hierarchy because there is so much at stake in higher education. Faculty members, however well intentioned, simply do not have the knowledge of the workings of the university to make the judgments that are often necessary at the institutional level. In this previously discussed situation about funding allocated to the IT unit, the faculty member needed to be silent and trust the academic leaders to be informed, honest, and dependable. This can be done at the chair level once effective collegial communication is freely established with the AVP. The AVP must assist the deans in creating the fundamental and essential collegial environment that supports decisions made for the greater *community* good. The key elements required to create a collegial culture include the following:

- The future of the department lies in the relationship of the chair with the AVP and the dean.
- Intelligent, well-chosen chairs are necessary to become effective leaders.
- Cipriano (2009) indicates that 85.8 percent of chairs want to make a difference, with 83.1 percent hoping to shape the department's future; this motivation should be capitalized on to bring forward productive, well-informed dissent.

- Open, authentic two-way communication
- Courage; AVPs need to be courageous in order to help deans and chairs to be so.
- Chairs can shape the legacy of their departments and programs.
- AVPs must inspire deans to be able to create the collegial environment necessary for chairs to be effective,
- There is a clamoring need for "productive dissent" possible only in a collegial culture.

Chair Can and Should Be Privy to Discussions as a Partner in the Academic Vision

In one college, faculty members were encouraged to apply directly to the president for small grants for creative initiatives. This inadvertently undermined the academic plan and role of the chief academic officer. This practice may also create favoritism and waste resources with faculty members currying favor with the office of the president. The monies were a small total of $10,000, with faculty members applying for awards of $1,500 or so for various projects. As the proposals were submitted, the president needed someone to manage the allocation so the director of human resources was asked to develop an application process and manage fund use. This was not new money but $10,000 taken out of the academic affairs base budget allocation. This resulted in faculty members applying to the director of human resources for monies more appropriately within the province of academic affairs. This funding opportunity was seen as just that: a chance for faculty members to obtain needed resources in a time of fiscal restraint. The end result was that initiatives once supported by the academic chief officer were now sponsored by the president. In such situations the AVP is then at risk for being perceived as not having the political clout to get initiatives implemented. This misalignment in structure,

My strength is a strong awareness and understanding of organizational structure and psychology. What good is this strength if not shared with others for the purposes of creating collegial institutions?

staff (the HR director), and values (no peer review) is a classic example of eroding the academic enterprise, controlling needed resources while seeming to support individual faculty members. The chair can be privy to this level of discussion as a partner in the vision for the future. There is no room for naiveté; a reality orientation is necessary and required. Collegiality means cooperative interaction among colleagues not just being civil.

Chair Not Being Consulted: Dire Consequences Due to Noncollegial Environment

In one college, the vice president of finance informed the faculty at an open forum that new faculty lines were opening up. This gave the impression that faculty lines lost through natural attrition were to be replaced. It simply should not be up to the finance officer to make this determination. Following the announcement of this good news, there was a scramble for replacement positions. If this were the way to fill faculty lines, the university of 2010 would look much like the university of 1976! Some faculty members and department chairs welcomed this seemingly innocent intrusion by the finance vice president because their own needs were met. I think back over the years to all the newer programs that have been established and shudder at the thought that they would not exist had fiscal allocation been determined without academic leadership. In my experience, the finance officer just finds it easier to keep track of new positions if the previous employee number is used as a tracking mechanism. So, faculty member number 111 left mathematics in 2001 and was never replaced so that spot is still available. Such programs as women's studies, recreation and leisure studies, exercise physiology, allied health studies, educational leadership, and many other programs would not have been created in the academy if this had been the modus operandi.

This anecdote about faculty line allocations illustrates how imperative it is for effective leadership to be inclusive in order to be collegial. This is not just a matter of civility but of survival. In a true community the AVP could and would inform the chairs of the true consequences of seemingly "good rewards," such as indiscriminately placed faculty lines. Within a true collegial partnership, the AVP can assist the chairs to understand that ultimately they will gain from more thoughtful shared allocation of resources. Wergin (2003) reminds us that we must think of the budget as a regional, coordinated effort and plan. This wasn't the case in this example: pulling faculty lines out of a hat to placate an increasingly cynical and retreating faculty. Such "godfather-like" rewards to a favored few are designed to diminish rather than enhance the autonomy of the academic enterprise. Only carefully crafted and thoughtful, inclusive leadership from the AVP can counter such seductive but poorly enacted favors from financial administrators. It is very difficult but ultimately worthwhile to engage chairs in part of the larger community of the institution. Academic endeavors will thrive best if individual components (structure, values, staff) are not misaligned and are in competition with one another. *Collegiality operationalized by the AVP shows respect for the common purpose, goals, and strategic plan of the department.*

Point of Service Effectiveness

The chair role is short on formal authority but support from the AVP in collaboration with deans can legitimize control at the point of service. *Point of service* represents language borrowed from health policy and leadership literature. The term connotes decision-making authority where it is most needed and effective; for example, at the interface with the client (patient, student, consumer, and so on) providers should be empowered to make decisions in accord with their ability, knowledge, and experience. Often this is not the case especially in hierarchical institutions such as the college and university. The following anecdote illustrates the need for point-of-service decision making in a familiar way that should resonate with all members of the academy. A director of continuing education met with me to advocate for a student. Apparently there were genuine extenuating circumstances requiring the student to abruptly withdraw from nonmatriculated course work. The university policy had a framework for decreasing amounts of reimbursement based on specific dates of withdrawal. This student life professional elaborated on the legitimate need to make an exception for this particular student with whom she had worked during her enrollment at the university. Eventually, she articulated such a strong case for a refund that I asked her why she was consulting me. The time certainly could be better used for other responsibilities for each of us. I stated this not in an adversarial manner but rather in puzzlement. Why not make this decision at the point of service, literally in the Office of Continuing Education? This is all part of collegiality as discussed earlier in this book. Chairs have been encouraged to share power, de-emphasize titles, and partake in other specific behaviors to create collegiality. This is also true for the AVP who must set the stage and requiring and supporting deans to do the same. In this instance the continuing education director should be treated as a mutually respected colleague, empowered to act competently within her area of responsibility. This represents a leap in faith in a new partnership with the unit leader at the point of service. It is a way of building collegiality and making sense of decision making through realignment.

Reiterated Strategies to Facilitate Collegiality Among All Reporting Structures Within Academic Affairs

- Share power and legitimate authority.
- Consult as colleagues.
- Take a leap in faith that will be a worthwhile payback for the institution.
- Provide information generously and appropriately.
- De-emphasize titles and differences.
- Be accessible.
- Be honest, competent, fair, credible, and dependable while treating all with dignity and respect.

I believe in the concept of "mentoring up" and as well as the more traditional notions of helping subordinates. The AVP has much to learn from deans, chairpersons, faculty, students, and the community. This can only occur in an environment developed around the collegiality described and examined in this book. The AVP can help the chair elicit help from others only by holding all reporting units responsible for a collegial environment. The AVP must make the chair a colleague, first and foremost, before helping the chair to make the department and program more collegial. This may represent a shift in leadership that requires bringing others into the mix. Expect a challenge from the "equal representation" proponents who are accustomed to the more traditional faculty committee structure. It is the responsibility of the AVP with the support of the deans and other appropriate administrators to make certain that suggestions outlined in Chapter Four regarding incivility are implemented and placed in the strategic plan. That there simply must be a cost to destructive behavior because it is hurtful to others and it bodes poorly for the future of the academic enterprises.

The AVP can support the chair to engage the faculty who seem to have pulled away from an institutional partnership. The academic leader has the responsibility of assisting the chair and the deans to encourage faculty efforts toward collective rather than individual efforts. It has been said that "a good faculty member is also a good university citizen" (Rosovsky, 1990, p. 165), but this is not true anymore. Newer and perhaps younger faculty members are not willing to give without compensation to the university enterprise. Their sense of loyalty is to their own careers rather than to any one institution. Higher education is almost a public utility; it serves a key role in economic utility and therefore must be able to demonstrate its contributions to the public good. A true collegial environment carefully nurtured can make these goals compatible rather than mutually exclusive. Faculty members in a collegial environment can be successful in the faculty role while engaging in the work of the broader institution and community.

It is a motivational challenge to successfully implement labor-intensive reform with faculty members who are already overburdened. In organization theory, such efforts fall under the rubric of organizational citizenship and discretionary effort, in which organizational members engage in self-sacrificing behaviors to achieve worthy goals for the greater good of the organization.

New Strategies for the Academy

To its credit, the academy has recognized these emergent trends and developed viable educational strategies to address them. In recent years the Association of American Colleges and Universities (AAC&U) has spearheaded an effort toward fundamental, student-centered circular reform. The result of this collaboration among faculty, administrators, accreditation agencies, and legislators has been most recently codified in *Greater Expectations: A New Vision for Learning as a Nation Goes to College* (AAC&U National Panel, 2002). This panel champions a renewed focus on student-learning outcomes to ensure that the undergraduate college experience will transform students so they can be more successful in life. Specifically, this experience should (1) prepare students with the knowledge and skills they need after college (for most this means securing a job and advancing in their career) and (2) give students the knowledge and skills they need to make a difference in their world by instilling a desire for intentional lifelong learning, community service, and social responsibility.

This new vision fundamentally expands and transforms the college curriculum across a variety of dimensions. If the efforts of the AAC&U are successful, professionalism as a college professor will be redefined to include, at a minimum, the following major educational themes in teaching and curriculum development:

- Learning communities
- Learning styles
- Interdisciplinary assessment

Misalignment

Although these new strategic approaches to higher education may be aligned with the needs of a changing educational environment, their effectiveness rests on whether or not they are actually implemented. Effective implementation will be challenged by misalignments with structure, staff, and value systems, all of which are currently in evidence in higher education.

Staffing and Value System Incongruities

Beyond a training deficit lies the problem of socialization in research-oriented doctoral programs. Doctoral students tend to self-select attendance at doctoral programs in research universities where they were socialized to aspire to research as the highest calling in academia (AAC&U National Panel, 2002; Barker, 2000):

- Public recognition, status, and institutional reputation tend to be linked with research output instead of teaching accomplishments.
- Gaining and maintaining accreditation by prestigious academic associations is often linked with consistent research accomplishment.
- Resources allocation from state legislatures, private foundations, and federal grant sources is usually tied to research productivity.

The moral of this story is simple and unlikely to change any time soon: research pays. In most universities and academic associations the path to prestige, status, accreditation, and resources is linked with research, not teaching accomplishments. Consequently, the pressure to hire the kind of research-oriented faculty members who impress accreditors and legislatures becomes increasingly intense. Even within many teaching institutions, rewards flow to the research-oriented faculty who bring in recognition, awards, grants, and other resources.

Faculty budget constraints leave minimal resources available to provide the training and coaching necessary to ensure that research-oriented new hires have the skills necessary to teach underprepared and nontraditional students. Most doctoral programs provide no formal training in teaching pedagogy.

As class loads increase and resource support decreases, the willingness of faculty to invest time and effort in intensive curricular reforms decreases as well, particularly among those research-oriented faculty members who are not trained in teaching pedagogy and would require extensive training to bring themselves up to speed. Without accreditation and documentation of student-learning outcomes, legislatures push for further resource constraints and the cycle repeats itself.

Rebuilding Alignment

So how does an institution convert faculty and administrators into supporting and participating in curricular reform that attends to the needs of increasing numbers of students? For faculty members with a high need for power who are not on the administration track, power is associated with internal resource allocation, external funding and grants, and leadership positions in academic and professional organizations. To the extent that educational reforms do not add to this power base, or worse, drain time and effort away from building further power and influence, such reforms are likely to receive lackluster support from this group.

Faculty

Many faculty members have a high level of achievement but they are not a homogenous group in defining what the nature of true academic achievement is. Although some define achievements as a combination of teaching and scholarship, others focus almost exclusively in terms of research. The following general guidelines provide faculty members with those elements of their job that are considered to be important.

- Prioritize student-centered learning activities that generate research and publication opportunities
- Prioritize interdisciplinary efforts that generate research and publication opportunities
- Prioritize initiatives and reforms that do not overburden faculty
- Prioritize education initiatives that support and make visible the strategic mission and distinctive competence of the institution

Implications and Conclusions

Despite the fact that the academy has identified the educational strategies needed to meaningfully address compelling environmental threats to higher education, the track record could be more encouraging. Misalignments among structures, staff, and value systems tend to undermine these strategic initiatives, despite their clear mandate from the outside environment (accreditation agencies, legislatures, foundations, and so on). Researchers warn that such misalignments have caused many curricular reform movements to flounder.

David Brenaman predicted in the prosperous 1990s that future financial challenges facing state governments would have dire consequences for public institutions of higher education (Guskin and Marcy, 2003). Costs are escalating in public and privates institutions beyond the ability of tuition revenues and fundraising efforts to cover them. What effect will ongoing significant budget reductions have on the quality of faculty work, life, and on student learning? This is a critical issue facing higher education. There may be a false sense of hope because most financial crises in higher education have been cyclical with always a better cycle merging. Strategies may temporarily help assuage the difficult financial constraints. Increased enrollment will lead to increased costs unless the delivery system is fundamentally changed. Attrition of aging faculty members seeking early retirement may help budget allocations for the short term by allowing replacement with less costly junior faculty.

Problems with the Role of Deans

Deans, the traditional academic leaders, have been lost to "survival mode." Deans are under pressure to increase enrollments, raise funds, and augment assessment and accreditation processes to please important stakeholders. They have been co-opted to "stay the course" until financial matters improve. Deans now send the message to the faculty via the chairs to "do more with less." But this approach can only work temporarily. Such measures may prove more harmful in the long run by masking the true nature and depth of the problems facing the viability of academic programs. Doing more with less will not work because the financial restraints are more serious and promise to be more permanent.

Difficult Lessons for Leaders

Deans may not be protecting their schools and programs but actually undermining the quality of the academic profession and of student learning. This is a difficult idea for leaders to grasp but an important one. The concept of enabling can be applied to higher education. I learned as an AVP that it was counterproductive to allow certain low-enrolled courses to run semester after semester. There were many admirable and valid reasons to continue some low-enrollment courses: contextual circumstances such as requirements for degree completion, core course sequencing, number of enrollees as imperfect indicator of course importance and quality, supporting curricular innovation by allowing new courses a chance to develop. These compelling reasons are shared by faculty members and must be part of the course cancellation decision making by academic leaders. However, on occasion, courses were permitted to run over a period of years with weak enrollments. Delaying the attention to these weak enrollment numbers may camouflage a real problem with program vitality. One computer science department failed to recognize that the academic offering was in jeopardy for this very reason; allowing courses to run despite steadily diminishing enrollments enabled the faculty to ignore the pipeline of declining students. The department needed to engage in a curricular audit and embark on a vigorous revitalization of the computer science program. Enabling courses to run with diminishing enrollments can hide the dramatic need for curricular revision. If the chair is carefully included in these serious conversation he or she will be open to reframing course delivery if the stakes are presented authentically. Who is better to visualize what the program should be in the next five years than the academic chair leader?

Doing More with Less: Why It Doesn't Work

Deans in one school reduced the academic coordinator credits in half so that faculty members received a 1.5 credit load per semester instead of the previous 3 credit load for coordinating academic programs. How long can this ruse be upheld before there is a decrease in quality and a diminished effort by an over-burdened faculty? The deans have become part of the problem in the sense that this credit reduction seems like a solution yet actually the faculty members' workload has been increased. Such tactics mimic the health care policy arena. Initial cost-control efforts are aimed at reducing the numbers of individuals served or eliminating some of the services offered yet decreeing that the program has not been cut! The deductible is often raised so that the policy holder does not know of the reduced offering of services until an attempt is made to use the service. The analogy in higher education is that the academic program still is being delivered but with a cost reduction. Eventually this looming budgetary dilemma must be faced. The academic chair is in the ideal position to voice this concern, especially if supported by the chief academic officer. The academic chair knows the program best and can begin to say no based on an informed rationale.

Deans also offered less credit for academic coordination in the summer, making alternative employment or nonemployment a more desirable alternative for the faculty. This risks the "good-citizen commitment" to the enterprise (Rosovsky, 1990) in a way that may never be recovered.

Deans were once the strong colleagues of the faculty and chairs. It may be that the deans are being blamed as victims because they may feel powerless to develop solutions in times of fiscal restraint. But it is not collegial to say "live with the cuts" to chairpersons who head academic programs. There must be better leadership than that. The solutions are in the very diffi-cult decisions to eliminate programs rather than have everyone suffer equally. Not to decide is to decide! Academe seems much better at delineating quality or unique programs but much less able, willing, or inclined to identify weaker programs or essential programs that could be delivered in more innovative ways.

Role of the Chair Living with Retrenchment

Retrenchment is a time when the chair once again comes to the fore. It must be decided which programs should be maintained and shored up in alignment with the vision for the department. Decisions are desperately needed to decide what to discontinue, modify, re-evaluate, or transfer to someone or something else: libraries, tutors, graduate assistants, IT personnel, preceptors, community partners, and so on. This first difficult and necessary step will lead to other transformative actions that will ultimately improve the program and the institution. Academic program components need not necessarily be eliminated but they surely cannot be sustained as is with constantly dwindling resources. The academic chairperson carefully chosen by peers, supported in the role, committed to excellence, in partnership with an informed chief academic officer, and freed to be a true colleague of the faculty is the logical and best hope for the future!

Honest, Effective Budgeting Key to Collegiality

Incremental budgeting represents weak leadership. A reduction across the board absolves leaders from needed decision making. If the budget stays essentially the same, what incentive is there to develop initiatives that address an improved vision? How the budget is allocated determines the future of the college or university. Nothing less is at stake. The AVP can work with the chair who will know what is needed and can understand what is at stake. Chairs will cooperate to the best of their ability when they share a genuine responsibility to create a better future.

Shared Leadership with the Chairs

Beatty and Page (2007) urge a leadership communication style that shares information openly and candidly throughout the organization. "In an environment where powerful constituencies with competing interests are constantly being tempted to turn communication into an opportunistic weapon, leaders must insist on the free and open sharing of authentic communication and accurate information from everyone involved."

Strategies to Suggest for Working with Chairs

Develop alignment around a vision of "what do we want the Recreation and Leisure Studies Department to look like in five years?" Rather than focusing on cancelling classes, using more adjuncts, counting travel, paper, and toner, the opportunity exists for genuine dialogue about the future of the program. This gives the chair the chance and the challenge to design a future for the program. Then the dean has the responsibility to rally the community and position the program with prospective students and stakeholders.

Redesign for an Upside-Down Alignment to Create Collegiality

An upside-down configuration represents a significant departure from past department structures that is timely and necessary. Deans don't determine department vision; the chairs do. The deans have a stronger instrumental role to bring the reconstructed programs to fruition. This critical realignment of staff, structure, and values must be done to save the academic enterprise. It is simply that important!

The deans can help to clarify what to pursue and what not to move forward. The across-the-board "tighten the belt" strategies are ineffective and demeaning to the work of the faculty and the institution and are destructive to collegiality, which should be the collective mission. One faculty colleague related a story about a school-level meeting called by the dean ostensibly to discuss strategic planning. The dean purportedly stated at a meeting, when speaking of the vision of the school, "I would like to see a master's degree certificate in gerontology." This statement was articulated in a manner independent of the very real issues of consolidation, program quality, diminishing resources, and faculty workload. This arbitrary recommendation may have been in response to the upper administration's call for ideas. Centers are attractive to legislative and other external stakeholders. This may seem like a good idea but it is nonsensical in isolation. This anecdote refutes the notion of collegiality. Congenial deans with administrative agendas contrary to good program sense can kill departments.

Beatty and Page (2007) argue that leaders should not develop visions to impart to their followers; instead, they encourage their followers to take initiative and develop visions to share with their leaders.

Use of Varied Campus Professionals to Develop Collegiality

In the strategies discussed in the literature to manage current and predicted financial restraints, there have been some very good suggestions about better alignment of staff that should be heeded. (Guskin and Marcy, 2003). Indeed, Beatty and Page (2007) applaud the more effective use of the many and varied campus professionals available to achieve strategic goals. The following represents a summary example of just such a successful multipersonnel effort to improve student learning at a public university. The author was coleader of a successful collaboration between student and academic affairs to start a first-year experience (FYE) in order to improve retention. This occurred a few years before such projects became ubiquitous at most colleges and universities and when there was a much clearer demarcation between the academic side of the house and student affairs. The collaboration was initially unwieldy, precarious, and subject to suspicion on both sides. A team of eight professors and student life professionals embarked on a pilot project to implement a cotaught and comanaged first-year student experience. The team presented the project at the 19th Annual Conference on the First-Year Experience (2001) titled, "Collaborative Partnerships Between University and Academic Affairs: A Model." This pilot was wildly successful just in terms of implementing an alternative delivery model with student life professionals coteaching with professors. The teaching teams advised students, mentored them, taught the classes, and evaluated the outcomes with the assistance of the Office of Management and Information Research (OMIR). After the first complete academic year of two semesters, the project collided with a bureaucratic snafu. The student life professionals were also considered full-time employees and were prohibited by contract from being compensated for teaching the course. The courses were mostly scheduled during the daytime because the target audience was the more traditional student who wanted the FYE classes during the prime day hours. The compensation could have been negotiated for evening classes because management employees of the university are permitted to teach in the evening. I am happy to think that all universities have come a long way since 2001 when such divisions in structures, roles, and responsibilities were commonplace and silos were impenetrable. It may seem incredulous but this proved initiative that had a better retention rate than the honors program at the university was scraped by the auditors. The structure at that time was so misaligned with academic outcomes that the best brains were not able to figure out how to permit a residence life professional with a master's degree to teach part of a course during the day.

Academe has a very long way to go despite much discussion of alternative delivery models and the very real investment in technology. No one had the legitimate power of leadership authority to make this happen. On an optimistic note, another FYE program was reinstated in 2007 but the coleaders are each professors from academic departments with varied campus professionals fully involved.

There are untoward risks in such realignment of roles and structure:

- Budget redistribution
- Blurring of accountability
- New and different but not improved territorial encroachment and turf wars

Inherently good is the intention of using other campus professionals in the teaching-learning process in addition to the traditional faculty. Despite this obvious merit, these efforts must include integrating an emerging and better faculty role and work life. This should not be a mere shift of traditional faculty responsibilities to capable others but a reevaluation of faculty productivity. There should be enough good will and resources to go around and not just tax the system in a different way. The goal should never be to marginalize, minimize, or diminish the faculty role in student learning but to enhance learning by capitalizing on all resources.

The possible negative consequences are serious and worth examination. The faculty can wind up with a diminished voice or an eroded role for the traditional academic chief officer and therefore the entire academic enterprise. The infusion of IT has enhanced our academic life beyond imagination, yet there are some risks. The temptation can be to focus on the technology rather than on the use of technology to improve student learning outcomes. The faculty can be complicit in this even if unwittingly.

Finally, we have an integrated delivery system. Most colleges and universities now have the technological capacity to coordinate admission, registration, finance, and other student services.

These departments were enhanced necessarily in the last two decades but must now be realigned. The restructuring of the academic delivery system to better use emerging technologies, lower costs, improve student learning, and support changing faculty roles must occur in tandem with the restructuring of administrative functions for the same shared purposes.

Search Process

The hope for the future is in the search process. This is easier said than done. My favorite hypothetical questions go something like this: We know that you have a PhD from Case Western Reserve but can you mentor undergraduate students? Would you be able to make a contribution to assessment of student learning? If so, how? The program is undergoing reaccreditation and expects a site visit in two years; what role do you see as a faculty member within the program in relation to this? Are you willing to coteach courses with graduate students or teaching assistants and IT personnel? What of a hybrid course development so that only half of the course is based on traditional class meetings?

Advisement That Really Enhanced the Chair Role in Unanticipated Ways

My experience has been that faculty members often complain about the labor-intensive nature of student advisement but are also reluctant to give it up. For altruistic motives, the faculty seem to cherish the traditional advisement role and perhaps for good reason. There is still an important need to advise students within the major and to meet one on one. But this is all very different than the blurred processes of registration, financial aid, and general advisement. These are better suited to the student life professionals who have the opportunity once again to restructure the role of the faculty. Historically, in some institutions, an inordinate amount of time was spent on advisement to the detriment of other aspects of faculty responsibilities. Recently, due to advances in technology we lifted much of the advisement out of the program level except for majors once accepted. Processes have shifted to online, Web-based registration and related student services. Ironically, once embedded in the student services area rather than as a faculty responsibility, there appears to be budget allocation for tracking software. The risk is always that as responsibilities shift so does the money. This is appropriate if justified by a true shift in role or in new base revenue streams. The risk is that the money will move to recruitment for ever-increasing enrollment purposes rather than back into ongoing program development with a revitalized, less-burdened faculty.

Successful Advisement Realignment

In a role as director (chair) of a program, I was able to hire a part-time, nonfaculty position similar to an administrative assistant for thirty hours per week. This addition of one person to serve as an information coordinator for the department dramatically altered the faculty role for the better. An honest appraisal determined that this personnel addition helped program delivery and the role of the department chair more than the addition of a full-time faculty line. This information coordinator has strong technological skills and carries out an array of activities that assist the program and relieve the faculty of administrative functions:

- Returns all phone calls
- Responds to all program inquiries
- Answers requests for brochures and other mailings
- Conducts information sessions
- Attends open houses
- Accompanies recruiters to meet with community stakeholders

These are mere examples of the activities that this individual performs but more important she serves as the liaison to admissions, registration, and financial aid. Other college professionals from these offices often e-mail with anticipation of immediate turnaround on various student issues involving payment, requirements, and transcripts. The faculty is not equipped to respond immediately due to other academic responsibilities. The expected immediate response from a faculty member to student service professional represents just one more misalignment within higher education. The information coordinator is better able to respond quickly because her responsibilities are more narrow than the faculty role. The unintended outcome is improved professional relations with these various support services coupled with the freeing up of faculty members for other necessary, academic matters.

Student inquiries were once local but now prospective students send out a blitz of applications even if not focused on our particular program. This is usual behavior simply because it is so easy to do. The new expectation is that a response should be forthcoming without delay. The information coordinator role has greatly increased the department's capacity to respond appropriately.

For the first time, the department can track the nature of the inquiry. Previously, the department simply did not have the human power to do this and worried about the proper use of faculty resources (time and effort) on such important but nonetheless additional tasks. The data make it easy for the information coordinator to know whether the interest is about varied subjects such as the following:

- International student opportunities
- Tuition reimbursement questions
- E-learning programs (can the program be completed entirely online?)

- Undergraduate versus graduate programs
- Doctoral program development in the future

Advisement redesigned around emerging technologies has greatly streamlined student services. *Again, this becomes an opportunity for the chair to lead.* In my experience, realigning of faculty work concerning advisement has created space for better examination of program delivery. There is now time and capacity to reevaluate the online programs that have proliferated but still require a full review. Despite a recent very successful accreditation review, the faculty must attend to the assessment of learning outcomes. Program quality maintenance requires ongoing discretionary effort, which is now possible. The chair was best able to forestall demand for an additional faculty member due to a strategic understanding of the priority needs of the department. The AVP supported the department in this unique restructuring of the program with an additional staff member for advisement. The vice president understood and trusted that the chair had the best "bird's eye view" to make such a recommendation.

Overuse of Electronic Communication

The chair may have had to put up with noncollegial, uncivil, disrespectful faculty members for far too long. Now add other college and university colleagues to the mix!

- The graduate student who e-mails a professor demanding to know why he did not receive an A grade
- Copies sent by blind copy feature to others through an inappropriate e-mail distribution list
- Demand for instant gratification; when e-mail not answered within twenty-four to forty-eight hours there is an escalation of messaging
- E-mails from students, colleagues, and university employees with spelling, grammar, and syntax errors . . . or shorthand

(BlackBerry speak) "U must answ rite away! I wk nites" stated one request from a student.

- Contacting the chancellor or board of trustees when a class limit is not expanded for increased enrollment

These examples represent exchanges that, sadly, are no longer uncommon in current institutions of higher learning. Overreliance on electronic communications represents a waste of resources because responses are sometimes required. The issue of uncivil communication indicates a lack of discrimination in style and decorum that does not bode well for academe.

The following factors contribute to the problem:

- Blurred boundaries; student and others in the community have access to contact information
- Ubiquitous e-mail and other electronic media hardware devices and software
- Informal language without titles
- Culture of immediate gratification
- E-mail copy distribution lists often do not contain titles or roles, just names, unlike cc: on letterhead, which provides name and role, for example, Dr. S. White, PhD, dean of Library.
- Unrealistic expectations lead to conflict and unresolved issues.
- Sense of entitlement incongruent with the reality of the faculty role

My professional life has been devoted particularly to defeating elitism in the academy; however, overly intimate, inappropriate, and inaccurate electronic communication is not an almighty leveler but rather a vulgarity that impedes genuine and necessary effective communication. Individuals can blurt out thoughts without proper filtering just because it is now possible.

Identifying Cyberbullying

When workforce violence policies were first established, there was a reluctance to use them, for example, "He only raised his voice and screamed at me so it really doesn't represent violence. I don't want to fill out a complaint form to human resources and get him into trouble." Such was a common response because workplace harassment was not defined and therefore stayed unrecognized.

Likewise, there is a cyber harassment continuum, even if not fully understood. Perhaps we can begin to conceptualize a continuum in an attempt to define and recognize what is acceptable (see Figure 6.1).

Receiving an e-mail copied to subordinates, administrators, strangers, and others within the institution without disclosing title or position is not acceptable and we need to state this clearly. I have often received an e-mail and wondered "who is J. Weatherman?" Does he or she work in financial aid or admissions? Why is he or she being copied? Should I respond back to all even though I do not know why they were copied in the first place? Is this the administrative assistant in the office? If so, the nature of the content would differ depending on to whom the message is delivered. This creates lost time and resources, unclear communication, risk of poor manners, and subsequent hurt feelings. And why? Just because we are able to do so as a benefit of technological capacity that we all share as modern employees. These examples of ineffective or injurious communication lead to problems going underground because many responses are not best delivered in memo form. To explain via e-mail may be too complicated and risks causing additional confusion and lack of clarity. The problem is that much necessary and authentic discussion is avoided. We should not accept that this is merely the

Figure 6.1 Continuum of Cyber Harassment Behavior

Courteous—demanding—rude—belligerent—increasingly hostile—threatening

way it is or a natural consequence of enhanced technological capability. Or should we handle this as a personal issue with each of us figuring out to respond to the ever-increasing volume and broadening nature of electronic communication. This e-mail bombardment is no longer a matter of personal management strategy but rather a systemic problem for the organization. The issue must be addressed effectively, firmly, and knowledgeably in a similar manner as our approach to sexual harassment.

Another example is of a part-time faculty member who thinks she has been paid less than a peer. She shoots off an e-mail implying unfair compensation and favoritism. Well, there are criteria that are used to determine pay scale for adjuncts including but not limited to

- Level of education
- Credentials
- Teaching experience
- Workload requirements

These policies and the compensation should be transparent and communicated in the hiring process; this is for certain. The e-mail under discussion can serve as an opportunity to highlight areas in which better communication of policies is needed. However, despite this unintended positive consequence, the problem of indiscriminate use of e-mail without any sanction is detrimental to collegiality. This is because collegiality must be grounded in trust, open and full exchange of information, and credibility. Enabling such low-level and harsh discourse is more than tolerating incivility; it is enabling a serious threat to the development of the shared community of scholars and must be addressed. This is a concern that cannot wait to be acted on because it represents a misalignment of structure and values so important to the long-term continued success of higher education.

Preventing Cyberbullying

Guidelines need to be determined by the faculty with the chair so that the communication with students and others remains collegial or aspires to collegiality. The policies must be clearly developed just like those for harassment or workplace violence. These must be included as policies in written bylaws of the department and then actively supported by deans, the AVP, and other administrators from essential service units. It is imperative that the faculty and the chair not feel powerless against inappropriate behavior, regardless of the source.

It is time to determine what cyberbullying looks like. What does it sound like? It is often tolerated because it is not fully recognized just as in the early days of awakening consciousness about other threats to collegiality: harassment and workplace violence. None of these are tolerated, so why tolerate incivility that borders on bullying, threatening, or rudeness? The search process must tease out an articulation of a willingness to work in a team environment as a cooperative venture. External consultants can be very helpful and necessary and should be a base allocation component of the AVP's budget. Institutions of higher education are complex organizations facing complicated issues that have high stakes for the future. Human resources should also be held accountable to function on behalf of the academic environment. Despite the advancement of human resource professionals and the improvement in these services in higher education, there are too many stories that indicate that the unit is not always welcoming to academic managers. I was recently surprised at the inability of a human resource unit to deal effectively with an impaired faculty member. My opinion is that human resources in the educational environment is just beginning to catch up to what is pro forma to comparably sized and comprehensive organizations that are not educational institutions. The HR department acted as if it were the first time that the institution had to address the issue of impaired behavior in an organization of two thousand employees and a one-hundred-year history. Comparable organizations, both private and public, have more advanced and nimble ways to immediately sanction, assist, and isolate such troubled individuals.

7

CASE LAW REGARDING COLLEGIALITY IN HIGHER EDUCATION

The Damage Done: Why Every Workplace Needs
the Rule

—*R. I. Sutton (2007)*

Chairs should be knowledgeable about what case law has determined relative to collegiality in higher education.

1. "Lack of collegiality" can be used as a basis to terminate a full-time faculty member.

2. Most institutions of higher education do not specify collegiality as a distinct criterion for tenure or promotion.

3. When considering the issue of collegiality in faculty employment decisions, courts of law have consistently upheld its importance.

4. Even though critics exist, courts have continued to uphold the use of collegiality as a factor in tenure and other higher education decisions in which First Amendment claims are raised.

5. The U.S. courts have ruled that the use of collegiality as a criterion for personnel decisions is not a breach of contract even though it has not been specified as a separate and distinct criterion in the faculty contract or handbook.

6. The U.S. courts have affirmed at every turn the use of collegiality as a factor in making decisions

concerning faculty employment, promotion, tenure, and termination.

7. Colleges and universities should feel confident in considering collegiality in faculty decisions and that it is unnecessary for them to specify it as a separate and distinct criterion.

8. Breach-of-contract argument: when factors of fitting in were not defined specifically as criteria for tenure, the U.S. courts stated that this does not violate employment or tenure policy.

9. Collegial behavior implies mindless conformity or total absence of dissent.

10. The courts do not perceive collegiality as important to the college or university to fulfill its missions.

11. A college or university has a right to expect a teacher to follow instruction and to work cooperatively and harmoniously with the head of the department.

12. Collegial relationships are most effective when peers work critically together to carry out their duties and responsibilities in the most professional manner possible.

13. Because of the very subjective nature of collegiality the courts should not substitute their judgment for that of faculty and administration.

14. "Professional collegiality" is not the same as "sociability" or "likeability."

15. Destructive conflict can immobilize departments.

16. A department chair is oftentimes left to fend for himself when trying to rein in a toxic faculty member.

The first fifteen statements are all true, except for statements number 8 and 9, which are false. Question number 16 can only be answered on a very personal and individual basis. Those chairs who have supportive deans and provosts as avuncular figures are quite fortunate. However, those chairs who are literally on their own in quelling the contagion of an uncivil, nasty person are in for a parlous existence!

"Does collegiality count?
While academics, legislators, and
board of trustee members debate
the relative importance of
collegiality in faculty personnel
decisions, the courts have clearly
and consistently spoken:
They will not protect truculent
professors!"

—M. A. Connell
and F. G. Savage (2001)

What the Courts Have Ruled—An Overview

Although there are many critics, the courts have continued to uphold the use of collegiality as a factor in tenure and other personnel decisions, and they have affirmed the use of collegiality as a factor in making decisions regarding faculty employment, promotion, tenure, and termination. Lack of civility or collegiality can be used as a basis to terminate a full-time faculty member. The courts have acknowledged all of the following in rendering their decisions relative to collegiality (Connell and Savage, 2001):

- Faculty do not operate in isolation; decisions such as curricula, class scheduling, and advising are made as a group.
- An ability to cooperate is relevant because of tenure.
- The courts perceive collegiality as important for universities to fulfill their missions.
- Universities do not have to specify collegiality as a specific criterion for personnel decisions.
- The courts have long deferred to university decisions regarding who should teach. They have continued to do so

when issues of collegiality and termination of tenured faculty have been involved.

- Because of the subjective nature of collegiality, courts should not substitute their judgment for that of faculty and administration.
- Because universities make a substantial commitment to the individual they should have wide discretion (that is, tenure is viewed as a lifetime appointment).
- The courts have concluded that collegiality, even when not specified as a separate evaluation criterion, is a relevant consideration in assessing teaching, research, and service.

Buller (2006) wrote that "to be sure, since collegiality affects the quality of a faculty member's teaching, scholarship, and service, it may well be regarded as an appropriate *implicit* factor— much as showing up for work on time and not plagiarizing another scholar's research are frequently unstated implicit criteria—when personnel decisions are made" (p. 50). Is it possible that a particular personality trait may make a faculty member a less effective teacher? Is the notion of "collegiality" so irrelevant after all in a department whose work depends heavily on consensus?

Most position descriptions for college and university faculty will include benchmarks subtly indicating concepts regarding collegiality. Many universities include within the teaching or service components of tenure and promotion documents a requirement that the candidate demonstrates an ability to "work well with colleagues," "show good academic citizenship," or "contribute to a collegial atmosphere." The department chair is primarily the person who assumes responsibility for monitoring these types of activities to faculty. Further, it is the job of the chair to determine whether faculty members measure up in these areas when tenure, promotion in rank, or reappointment decisions are made.

Question: "Should collegiality be a separate criterion in tenure decisions?"

* * *

Answer: "Collegiality *should* be a separate criterion in tenure decisions but the real question is whether or not this is truly feasible. The answer will ultimately lie in case law. I am aware that there have been decisions that have supported the denial of tenure on the bass of a lack of collegiality but am unsure whether the existing case law is sufficient to support such an action in other situations. I would be reluctant to include collegiality as a tenure criterion without this assurance." —Sue Ouelette, chair, Department of Communicative Disorders, Northern Illinois University

Answer: "I have mixed emotions about the use of the 'collegiality' variable when making important decisions about tenure, promotion, and merit decisions. As important as collegiality is within a unit, it could also be used unfairly by a cohort of faculty members who may 'have it out' for a particular colleague. I have managed a department in which a particular faculty member's behavior was evaluated quite poorly by several of his or her peers on a regular basis, but he or she was well liked and appreciated by a few faculty outliers who were not as outspoken as the others. A chair must be aware of the inappropriate, and potentially unfair, use of collegiality ratings by peers." —Stuart J. Schleien, professor and director of graduate study, Department of Recreation, Tourism, and Hospitality Management, University of North Carolina at Greensboro

Answer: "In addition to the traditional teaching, scholarship, and service duties of faculty they must also be held accountable for collegiality. In our job announcements and in the interview we emphasize not only our expectations for

(*continued*)

(*continued*)

excellence in teaching, research, and scholarship, but also the 'ability to work in a team environment.' " —Walter H. Gmelch, dean, School of Education, University of San Francisco

Answer: "Yes, I would like to see collegiality as an identified criteria for tenure." —William F. Williams, provost and vice president for academic affairs, Slippery Rock University

Answer: "I believe collegiality should be a separate criterion for tenure." —Bruce W. Russell, dean, College of Business, Information, and Social Sciences, Slippery Rock University

In October 2010 I sent a survey to 286 chairs across the country. A total of 104 chairs responded to the survey: a 36.4 percent return rate. One of the questions on the survey asked, "Should collegiality be the fourth criterion, in addition to teaching, scholarship, and service, for tenure decisions?" Respondents were asked to check only one of the following answers: yes, no, or not sure. The results show the following:

- Seventy-six chairs (73.1 percent) indicated that yes, collegiality should be a separate criterion for tenure decisions.
- Twelve chairs (11.5 percent) indicated that no, collegiality should not be a separate criterion for tenure decisions.
- Sixteen chairs (15.4 percent) indicated that they were not sure if tenure should be included as a separate criterion for tenure decisions.

I have been invited to visit many institutions of higher education, from community colleges to Research 1 universities, since about 2005. Specifically, I have provided seminars and workshops to department chairs and deans relative to collegiality. In my experience, fully 90 percent of the attendees indicate that they would like to see collegiality as a separate criterion for tenure decisions.

The Courts' Decisions

Courts have long deferred to decisions of universities regarding who should teach and they continued to do so even when issues of collegiality and termination of full-time, tenured faculty have been involved. Courts perceive collegiality as important to the ability of universities to fulfill their missions. In most cases collegiality has not been specified as a separate evaluation criterion. However, in spite of this, courts have still concluded that collegiality is a relevant consideration in assessing teaching, research, and service. Given the strength and unanimity of the case law, institutions of higher education can feel confident from a legal standpoint in considering collegiality in faculty employment decisions, even if it is not specified as a separate and distinct criterion. However, some universities do recognize the importance of collegiality in awarding tenure. Auburn University in Alabama has a policy on collegiality for tenure decisions.

Tenure Criteria and Considerations

Auburn University (2011) nurtures and defends the concept of academic tenure that ensures each faculty member freedom, without jeopardy at the department, college, school, or university level, to criticize and advocate changes in existing theories, beliefs, programs, policies, and institutions and guarantees faculty members the right to support, without jeopardy, any colleague whose academic freedom is threatened. Tenure establishes an environment in which truth can be sought and expressed in one's teaching, research and creative work, outreach work, and service. Decisions on tenure are different in kind from those on promotion. Tenure, in fact, is more exacting. In addition to demonstrating quality in the areas of (1) teaching, (2) research and creative work, (3) outreach, and (4) service as described under promotion criteria, the candidate for tenure must also demonstrate professional collegiality.

Collegiality

In appraising a candidate's collegiality, department members should keep in mind that the successful candidate for tenure will assume what may be an appointment for thirty years or more in the department. Collegiality should not be confused with sociability or likeability. Collegiality is a professional, not personal, criterion relating to the performance of a faculty member's duties within a department. The requirement that a candidate demonstrate collegiality does not license tenured faculty to expect conformity to their views. Concerns relevant to collegiality include the following: Are the candidate's professional abilities and relationships with colleagues compatible with the departmental mission and with its long-term goals? Has the candidate exhibited an ability and willingness to engage in shared academic and administrative tasks that a departmental group must often perform and to participate with some measure of reason and knowledge in discussions germane to departmental policies and programs? Does the candidate maintain high standards of professional integrity.

Collegiality can best be evaluated at the departmental level. Concerns respecting collegiality should be shared with the candidate as soon as they arise; they should certainly be addressed in the yearly review and particularly the third-year review. Faculty members should recognize that their judgment of a candidate's collegiality will carry weight with the promotion and tenure committee.

Question: "How difficult is it to add collegiality to promotion and tenure criteria?"

*   *   *

Answer: "It is certainly not easy . . . or quick. There are many variables that affect adding collegiality to tenure and promotion documents: union versus nonunion campus, transparency of administration, trust built throughout the university, faculty buy-in, strength of faculty senate, how it is presented (that is, faculty driven versus administration driven), and so on. There must be open dialogues held in concert with shared governance and academic freedom principles. Every faculty member—tenured as well as nontenured—must have opportunities to speak for or against it. Also, it is very important that objective standards be applied to this factor so that there is no vagueness or ambiguity of what, in fact, constitutes collegiality." —Robert E. Cipriano, professor emeritus, Department of Recreation and Leisure Studies, Southern Connecticut State University

The 1999 statement of the American Association of University Professors "On Collegiality as a Criterion for Faculty Evaluation" points out that collegiality is not a distinct capacity to be assessed independently of the traditional triumvirate of scholarship, teaching, and service. Therefore, according to this document, its capacity lies not in defining it as a singular factor of status but instead in the virtue of its definition in support of the work of faculty in the areas of scholarship, teaching, and service (AAUP, 1999). Generally speaking, professors are erudite and possess those qualities that will allow meaningful standards to be developed and that will enable criteria to be written objectively regarding collegiality. Universally approved safeguards must be followed in a highly transparent way so that the

university community is in agreement and supportive of this initiative. It must be clear to all that a policy to include collegiality
as a fourth criterion in tenure decisions is not a form of retribu-
tion or payback but one of many ways for a university to be more
civil and collegial. Idiosyncratic behavior, long a hallmark in
academe, will still exist. People will still remain outspoken in
their thoughts and beliefs. What will change, it is hoped, will be
that normal discourse will be held in a respectful manner. I am
not naive enough to believe that merely adding collegiality as a
criterion to tenure decisions will automatically make noxious
people nice. I do concur with Owens (2004) that there is a need
to develop a culture that not only places a high value on but also
supports and enhances openness, high trust, caring, and sharing;
that strives for consensus but supports and values those who
think differently; and that prizes human growth and development above all. Buller (2010) wrote that "there's absolutely no
reason why even senior employees or tenured faculty members
cannot be reprimanded or dismissed for poor interpersonal
skills, a lack of collegiality, or simply an inappropriate 'fit' with
the evolving needs of the institution. That conclusion must,
however, be based on documented instances of behaviors
that cause problems, not on something as intangible as a vague
'perception' " (p. 2).

Professional Rights and Responsibilities

The Connecticut State University-AAUP *Collective Bargaining
Agreement* states that "as colleagues, professors have obligations that derive from common membership in the community
of scholars. They respect and defend the free inquiry of their
associates. In the exchange of criticism and ideas they show
due respect for the opinions of others. They acknowledge their
academic debts and strive to be objective in their professional
judgment of colleagues" (CSU-AAUP and Board of Trustees,
2007–2011, p. 12).

Auburn University is not the only institution of higher education that has a defined policy regarding collegiality. Northern Illinois University (2008) has adopted the following policy concerning the use of collegiality.

University Collegiality Policy

1.1 Preamble

1.11. Collegiality represents a reciprocal relationship among colleagues with a commitment to sustaining a positive and productive environment as critical for the progress and success of the university community. Collegiality is a multidimensional construct that permeates the successful execution of all parts of the tripartite: scholarship, learning, and service. It consists of collaboration and a shared decision-making process that incorporates mutual respect for similarities and for differences in background, expertise, judgments, and points of views, in addition to mutual trust. Central to collegiality is the expectation that members of the university community will be individually accountable to conduct themselves in a manner that contributes to the university's academic mission and high reputation. Collegiality among associates involves constructive cooperation and engagement in academic and administrative tasks within the respective units and in relation to the institutional life of the university as a whole. Collegiality is not congeniality or is it conformity or excessive deference to the judgments of colleagues and administrators; these are flatly oppositional to the free and open development of ideas. Evidence of collegiality is demonstrated by the protection of elementary principles of academic freedom, the capacity of colleagues to carry out their professional functions without obstruction, and the

(continued)

(*continued*)

ability of a community of scholars to thrive in a vigorous and collaborative intellectual climate.

1.12. Northern Illinois has a tradition of collegiality and shared governance and strives to maintain that as a mainstay of its institutional culture. The preamble to the Northern Illinois Constitution declares "respect for the intrinsic dignity of each member of the university community, both by the university itself and by each member of that community, is the basic cornerstone governing all community activities." This university is a community whose varied functions, responsibilities, and contributions are supportive of the instructional, research, and service missions of the institution. Collegial interactions as referenced throughout this policy are those interactions that occur among and between colleagues, subordinates, supervisors, administrators, and students. Collegial interactions are essential to support that mission in an effective, efficient, and ethical manner.

1.13. Allegations or complaints of a documented pattern of frequent and pervasive uncollegial activity, or a severe uncollegial act, if found to be supported, will constitute a violation of this policy. Such allegations will be examined in a reasonable, objective, and expedient manner and in accordance with applicable federal and state employment laws. This policy is intended to be consistent with the preamble to Article 11 of the Northern Illinois *Bylaws*, which states, "Therefore, it is crucial for the university to ensure the right of all faculty and staff (supportive professional and operating staff) to perform their individual and collaborative roles in an environment that is free from incivility, misuse of authority, intimidation, retaliation, and infringement on personal and academic freedom."

1.2. Disposition of Complaints

1.21. The consequences of uncollegial activity may be the creation of a chilly or hostile environment that alters the conditions of the employment and academic environment. Unlike discrimination or harassment, uncollegial activity does not need an identified target to have a negative impact on the employment and academic environment. Or does an occasional comment or unprofessional action constitute uncollegiality unless such conduct is severe, pervasive, or occurs on a frequent basis.

1.22. Any administrator, faculty member, staff member, or student who experiences or witnesses possible uncollegial conduct has the right to report this activity and all supporting evidence to the applicable university administrator, especially if the effect of the conduct could be shown to have created an intimidating, hostile, or obstructive work environment.

1.23. The university encourages the maintenance of a positive employee-relations environment that includes effective communication and feedback and attempts to informally resolve complaints. The university strongly encourages the resolution of issues through informal procedures, beginning at the lowest appropriate level. Initial attempts will usually include discussions with those alleged to have committed the action or conduct. A request for mediation may be made to the office of the appropriate dean or the executive vice president and provost. The mediation process is a voluntary process that provides an avenue for the parties to discuss their workplace issues or concerns with each other directly, as facilitated by a trained mediator. The agreement by the parties to engage in mediation will stay any formal disciplinary process that may result from the allegation of a violation. On the successful resolution of the

(continued)

(*continued*)

mediation, the matter is concluded per the terms of the mediation.

1.24. In the absence of a successful mediation resulting in resolution, the allegation or complaint may be submitted for formal examination according to the university's grievance procedures for faculty and staff, *Bylaws*, "Article 11," in which a documented pattern of frequent and pervasive uncollegial activity shall be treated as "the grievable act," unless the complaint alleges a single but severely uncollegial act. The failure to act within thirty days of the failed mediation concludes any further consideration of the allegations or underlying conduct.

Language drawn from *Bylaws*, "Article 11: Grievance Procedures for Faculty and Staff."

Language drawn from *Affirmative Action and Diversity Resources (AADR)*, "Non-Discrimination/Harassment Policy and Complaint Procedures for Employees and Students." [www.nie.edu/aadr/policy.pdf].

AADR, 1 *Bylaws*, "Article 11, Item 11.4"; language in the fourth sentence is drawn from the *Bylaws*, "Article 10, Item 10.2." [www.niu.edu/u_council/attachments/2008–2009/Univcolpolicy.html].

Universities and the Courts

Connell and Savage (2001) present the following case histories of collegiality issues. In 1972 in *Chitwood* v. *Feaster*, the court found that a college has a right to expect a professor to work cooperatively and cordially with the department head. The court further indicated that there were expectations that a professor would follow instructions put forth by the department head. Collegiality was not the focus of court decisions until 1981, when the Court of Appeals for the Fourth Circuit in *Mayberry* v. *Dees* introduced into higher education case law the defined concept of *collegiality* as a distinct criterion on which to base tenure and promotion decisions. Outside the academy, a person's ability to work with others in a civil, positive manner is taken into account when personnel decisions are made. Why should the academy be different? This question may be self-evident based on a national survey conducted between 2005 and 2007 for the Collaborative on Academic Careers in Higher Education (COACHE), a research center at the Harvard Graduate School of Education. According to the data obtained by COACHE, a collegial department figures heavily in faculty satisfaction, ahead of the institution's work and family policies, ahead of clear tenure policies, and even ahead of compensation. Cathy Trower (2008), COACHE director, shared that "our findings suggest that campuses can greatly increase the odds of attracting and retaining top junior faculty by paying attention to climate in departments. How are junior faculty treated? Does everyone have access to important collaborations with senior colleagues. Are young faculty well-mentored?" (p. 7).

Breach of Contract Argument

The most persistent argument raised by faculty who were denied tenure because of a lack of collegiality is that the university's consideration of his or her personality, collegiality, or "fitting in" during the tenure evaluation violated either the employment contract or the institution's tenure policy because those factors were not specifically defined as part of the criteria for tenure. The question is, Does this violate employment for tenure policy? The U.S. Courts have ruled that this does not, in fact, violate tenure policy (*University of Baltimore* v. *Peri Iz*, 1993). The Maryland Court of Special Appeals indicated that collegiality is a valid consideration for tenure, even though it is not expressly listed among the university's criteria for tenure. The reason for this ruling is that collegiality is impliedly embodied within the criteria that are specified (that is, teaching and service).

First Amendment Argument

Arguments raised by faculty who were denied tenure state that the refusal to grant tenure based on collegiality issues represents a callous attempt to suppress lawful speech. Further, the First Amendment clearly prohibits public officials (that is, the university) from retaliating against those who engage in unpopular or offensive speech. This is considered to be germane in the university setting in view of the fact that the Supreme Court has made clear that First Amendment freedom must be vigilantly protected. However, the courts have continued to uphold the use of collegiality as a factor in tenure and other higher education employment decisions in which First Amendment claims are raised.

Ability to Cooperate

In *Bresnick* v. *Manhattanville College*, the courts ruled that "it is predictable and appropriate that in evaluating service to an institution, ability to cooperate would be deemed particularly relevant where a permanent, difficult-to-revoke long-term job commitment is being made to the applicant for tenure" (Connell and Savage, 2001, p. 39).

Discrimination Claims

In *Stein* v. *Kent State University*, the courts ruled that "the ability to get along with co-workers, when not a subterfuge for discrimination, is a legitimate consideration for tenure decisions." (Connell and Savage, 2001, p. 39).

Maintenance of a Collaborative and Cooperative Community

Few, if any, responsible faculty members would deny that collegiality, in the sense of collaboration and constructive cooperation, identifies important aspects of a faculty member's overall performance. A faculty member may legitimately be called upon to participate in the development of curricula and standards for the evaluation of teaching, as well as in peer review of the teaching of colleagues. Much research, depending on the nature of the particular discipline, is by its nature collaborative and requires teamwork as well as the ability to engage in independent investigation. And committee service of a more general description, relating to the life of the institution as a whole, is a logical outgrowth of the Association's view that a faculty member is an "officer" of the college or university in which he or she fulfills professional duties. [American Association of University Professors, 1999, p. 39.]

Collegiality Statements—Selected Universities

The following examples are all drawn from Mary Ann Connell and Frederick Savage (2001).

Arizona State University has the following policy regarding collegiality: "Service to university includes individual's expected contributions to internal committee work, faculty governance activities, and preservation of collegial atmosphere at all levels of interaction within the university" (p. 37).

The University of Florida indicates that faculty members need to "contribute to orderly and effective functioning of academic unit . . . act in a collegial manner in all interactions" (p. 40). Their stated policy includes compatibility and collegiality in factors to be considered in layoffs.

The University of Texas's policy concerning collegiality stated that the "future of academic institutions and education received by its students turn in large part on collective abilities and collegiality on the school's tenured faculty" (p. 40). Their policy reinforces the ability to cooperate as particularly relevant when long-term grant of tenure is involved.

"As colleagues, professors have obligations that derive from common membership in the community of scholars. Professors do not discriminate against or harass colleagues. They respect and defend the free inquiry of associates. In the exchange of criticism and ideas professors show due respect for the opinions of others. Professors acknowledge academic debt and strive to be objective in their professional judgment of colleagues. Professors accept their share of faculty responsibilities for the governance of their institution."

—AAUP Statement of Professional
Ethics (1987)

Creating a Collegial Department

In the unique role of serving as the connecting link between faculty members and management, department chairs are often requested to respond to the following questions regarding collegiality:

- Should the ability to "get along," "fit in," or "work well" with one's colleagues be a requirement for tenure?
- Should collegiality be a separate factor in tenure decisions or should it be considered as a part of the evaluation of teaching, research, and service?
- Is the university professor supposed to be a congenial coworker or a competent professional— or to a degree both?
- In your department, can collegiality serve as a means for concealing discriminating treatment of others who are not like us?
- Does a "winning personality and smile" count more in your department than quality teaching, superior research, or desirable service to the department?

How Is Collegiality Reflected in Your Department?

In judging any individual for reappointment, merit pay increase, tenure, or promotion, how important are the following factors in the future success of the individual? And how much potential do they have to greatly affect the work of the department?

- Collaborative work
- Positive attitudes
- Flexibility
- Positive interpersonal relationships within the university community
- Demonstration of appropriate levels of responsibility with respect to one's work in the university

There is a growing interest in how factors such as these serve to support a setting in which one's department is the primary focus of a faculty member's work. We look to one another as colleagues who are expected to conduct ourselves professionally in support of our students and each another.

Accepting and sharing responsibility for creating a productive work setting within the department and university is viewed in terms of how well we carry our fair share of the workload. The challenges faced by universities in the twenty-first century cannot be successfully mastered or can the efforts of dedicated professionals be sustained when attitudes and dispositions of personnel within departments are divisive, uncompromising, and inflexible or reflect a lesser degree of personal responsibility around a unified purpose. I am talking about the importance of that salient, fundamental hallmark of successful interactions in academe that we call *collegiality*.

Collegiality is reflected in the relationships that emerge within departments. It is often evidenced in the manner in which members of the department show respect, interact with each other, and work collaboratively with a common purpose in mind. Thus in those instances when it is held in high esteem, it may confidently be said that collegiality is the cornerstone of professional work. Yet in other settings the importance attached to it lacks clarity, as evidenced by the range of opinions and responses it receives in discussion. In short, it has been celebrated in some settings, undermined in others, and in still other places completely overlooked and ignored.

One might conclude that we attach different meanings to the ideas of collegiality and that raises the specter that this desired state of interaction is an unattainable idea that cannot be objectively measured. As a result, one is led to question how to clarify personal and collective perspectives surrounding the nature of this generally acclaimed state of professional interaction.

Collegiality Recap

Lack of collegiality can be used as a basis to terminate a full-time faculty member. The courts have acknowledged that

- Faculty do not operate in isolation; decisions (for example, curricula, class scheduling, advising, and so on) are made as a group.
- An ability to cooperate is relevant because of tenure.
- Collegiality is important to the ability of universities to fulfill their mission.
- Universities do not have to specify collegiality as a specific criterion for personnel decisions.
- Courts have long deferred to university decisions regarding who should teach. They continue to do so when issues of collegiality and termination of tenured faculty have been involved.
- Because of the subjective nature of collegiality, courts should not substitute their judgment for that of faculty and administration. Basically, it is an *academic exercise*.

- Because universities make substantial commitment to the individual they should have wide discretion; tenure is viewed as a lifetime appointment.
- The courts have concluded that collegiality, even when not specified as a separate evaluation criterion, is a relevant consideration in assessing teaching, research, and service.

Although critics exist, the courts have continued to uphold the use of collegiality as a factor in tenure and other employment decisions. They have consistently and constantly affirmed the use of collegiality as a factor in making decisions regarding faculty employment, promotion, tenure, and termination.

History

You are the chair of a department of fifteen full-time faculty members. You have been at the university for eighteen years and have the rank of full professor. When the chair in your department retired, the dean asked you to serve as the permanent chair. Your colleagues in the department overwhelmingly supported this decision and strongly encouraged you to take this leadership opportunity. After much soul searching you accepted the position. This is your second year serving as chair. You replaced a person who served as chair for seven years, Dr. Vitiello. However, Dr. Vitiello was just going through the motions during the last two years of his appointment; he was clearly waiting to retire. You learned very quickly on taking over as chair that a great deal had slipped through the cracks during that time.

Dr. Williams is an untenured assistant professor in his third year in the department. Other faculty colleagues have indicated that Dr. Williams is unwilling to collaborate on projects and does not take constructive criticism well. Last year you witnessed his obdurate behavior numerous times.

CASE STUDY

CASE STUDY

On two separate occasions he aimed a profane fusillade at undergraduate students who were questioning him about the grade they received on an assignment. This caused a kerfuffle in the class he was teaching and consequently many students dropped the course. He has made astringent and personal remarks to his faculty colleagues on occasion. His teaching evaluations from students are very inconsistent.

Problem

There are four ratings used to assess nontenured faculty members for reappointment: not recommend, recommend, highly recommend, and very highly recommend. In Dr. Williams's reappointment evaluation last year, you rated to "recommend" him for another year. Although you did recommend his reappointment, this is the second lowest evaluative measure you could give him. In your anecdotal comments you did, in fact, make specific mention of the fact that he is often noncollegial and disrespectful and demeaning to students, faculty peers, and professional staff. You counseled him to become more ubiquitous, respectful, and collegial. You also advised him to be less lugubrious, rancorous, and injudicious. This year you made a decision to not recommend Dr. Williams for reappointment. The implication of this decision is that he will be terminated from his position.

Response

Dr. Williams, on learning of his impending dismissal, obtained the services of an attorney. Through his attorney, he threatens to sue both you and the university. He indicates that the former chair, Dr. Vitiello, completed his reappointment evaluation and his decision was to *highly recommend* his reappointment. Further, there was nothing written in the section for anecdotal comments by Dr. Vitiello. You clearly have a dilemma: on the one hand, you do not want this person to continue to remain in your department; on the other hand, you do not want a lawsuit. What do you do?

Possible Solution

First and foremost, this is not your problem to deal with by yourself. You should schedule a meeting with the dean and provide her with all relevant information. Testimony from faculty, students, and staff regarding the parlous behavior that Dr. Williams has displayed should be provided. Pertinent notes that you have taken should also be presented, along with the previous reappointment appraisal documents. You and the dean should enlist the help and advice of key people at the university, for example, attorney(s), human resources, the union (if applicable), the state's attorney general's office (if applicable), and so on. It is very unfortunate that the previous chair did not perform his due diligence in assessing Dr. Williams in a careful, thorough, and objective manner. However, it is instructive to note that the United States courts have constantly and consistently affirmed the use of collegiality as a factor regarding faculty employment, tenure, and termination.

CASE STUDY

Conclusion

There certainly has been a great deal of discussion within the academic community, some passionate and most forthright and strident, over the use and possible abuse of collegiality in higher education employment decisions. Those who support the use of collegiality make the following arguments:

- There is a legitimate and longstanding expectation that faculty will work together in a cooperative manner in the best interests of the institution.
- This expectation is a reasonable part of all employment decisions in the private business world and should be the same within the academy.

- The courts have consistently given overwhelming support to the consideration of collegiality.

- The most frequent argument raised against the use of collegiality is that it is a breach of contract for a college or university to consider collegiality unless it has been specified as a separate and distinct criterion in the faculty contract or handbook. Faculty members who have been denied tenure or who have been terminated for a lack of collegiality have also asserted that because it is such a vague or ambiguous term, it can be easily used as a pretext for discrimination. The AAUP has argued that the use of collegiality as a factor in faculty employment decisions poses a real danger to academic freedom and free speech.

With respect to the breach of contract argument, courts have unanimously rejected that claim, regardless of whether the institution specified collegiality as a separate criterion or it did not. Courts have concluded that collegiality is implicitly embodied in consideration of the traditional criteria of teaching, research, and service. When addressing the assertion that the use of collegiality can be used as a pretext for discrimination, the courts have recognized that this can indeed take place. However, in the overwhelming number of reported cases dealing with such an allegation, the courts have rejected the claim that collegiality was used as a pretext and have upheld college and university decisions based on a lack of collegiality. Finally, although the courts have taken seriously assertions that the use of collegiality was a violation of academic freedom or free speech, they have held in favor of the college or university in the great majority of cases, finding often that the faculty member's conduct in question involved petty, personal disputes not protected by the First Amendment. Institutions of higher education should feel confident in considering collegiality in faculty decisions and that it is not necessary for them to specify collegiality as a separate and distinct criterion.

Conclusion

The department chair position is an extraordinary, albeit challenging, job in higher education. Historically the chair has played a pivotal role in serving as a change agent, not only in her department but also in the university as a whole. It is an exciting position because a chair can provide leadership to initiate new curricula changes, set in motion a new direction for the department, hire and mentor young faculty, and so on. A chair's responsibilities—and challenges—seem endless but the position is ill-defined. Chairs realize that they are not really members of the administration in the true sense of the word. Also, they are cognizant that they are not really faculty members. They are a hybrid person-in-the-middle who comes to the job without any specific education or training in performing the duties that he or she is asked to regularly perform. The majority of chairs are required to teach classes, conduct research, serve on committees, advise students, mentor faculty members, develop and implement a department budget, make critical personnel decisions, serve as the liaison between the administration and the department, and so on. The expectations are enormous, and growing exponentially. People who are drawn to this noble position do so in order to make a difference.

There has always been discord and lack of collegiality within academe, dating back to Harvard College in 1636. The U.S. courts have affirmed at every turn the use of collegiality as a factor in making decisions concerning faculty employment, promotion, tenure, and termination. However, despite this support from a legal standpoint, the lack of civility currently permeating institutions of higher education appears to be at a breaking point. Lack of collegiality, nastiness, and toxicity are causing many department chairs to seriously rethink their current position. The annihilating behavior of one toxic person can cause a furious sandstorm or tsunami obliterating everything and everyone in his path. Department conflicts metastasize as resentments fester and scapegoats are sought. Demagogues inevitably emerge to feast on the poisonous stew of such an environment.

We do know that conflict is inevitable—it is the natural outcome of human interaction. Chairs establish the tone for a healthy climate and maintain a positive culture in the department. The department chair plays a major and important role in managing conflict within the department. The chair is oftentimes left in the unenviable position of being singularly responsible for reining in a toxic faculty member. This simply will not work, especially if this noxious person is tenured. If this detritus is allowed to continue the department will become a dystopia. Chairs should not be left to single-handedly deal with an uncivil, disrespectful, and noncollegial faculty member. A department chair should be viewed as one of many university constituencies that work collaboratively to rein in an uncivil person. The most effective approach is one that addresses the concerns of incivility, noncollegiality, and lack of respect in a systematic manner. There should be university-wide policies and procedures established that promote collegiality, civility, and respect campuswide. The time of oscillating between either actively acknowledging that malefactors—feckless, vitriolic, and rancorous faculty members—render departments dysfunctional or treating them with solicitude should be over. It is axiomatic that a lack of civility, collegiality, and respect should not be tolerated. The department chair needs the support of the university's vast on-campus resources (human resources, counseling department, law school, faculty senate, and so on), all members of the university community (faculty, professional staff, and students), as well as the assistance of the central administration (deans, provost, and president). As chairs we should strive for nothing less than civility and respect in our daily encounters with our colleagues. Anything less will besmirch the noble role of the department chair. After all, in the final analysis, don't we all strive to be respected and treated with civility?

Appendix

A FOUR-YEAR STUDY
OF DEPARTMENT CHAIRS

Since 2007, my colleague Richard Riccardi and I have been surveying department chairs throughout the country to help define who they are, what they do, what they are expected to do, and ultimately, what drives them to want to be in their current position. The survey-questionnaire was designed to bring out responses about demographics (for example, age, gender, rank, how they became chair, and so on), personal information (for example, satisfaction in the chair role, what they will do after serving as chair, and so on), perceptions of the skills and competencies needed to effectively function as chair, and their reflections on the pleasant or unpleasant nature of the tasks chairs need to perform. Each year, the study has evolved as analysis of the current year's data has brought to light deeper and more complex issues; as research often does, our "answers" to specific questions have resulted in more thought-provoking questions.

In 2007, we surveyed a state university system on the past, present, and future aspirations of department chairs (Cipriano and Riccardi, 2008) and found that department chairs set their own expectations at almost unrealistic levels: a "master of all trades." In 2008, we broadened the survey in scope and distance (Cipriano and Riccardi, 2010a), surveying chairs from across the country about their satisfaction levels and reasons why they stay as department chairs. In this study, we were puzzled to find that more than 85 percent were either satisfied or very satisfied serving as chair, yet the number-one reason they remain in their position is that "no one else will do it." Further qualitative research resulted in modifications to the 2008 survey instrument when focus groups with chairs brought to light that "making a difference" was a key factor in becoming a department chair. Therefore, as part of the 2009 study (Cipriano and Riccardi, 2010b) comparing current and former chairs, the following answers to the question of why people remain as chair were added: (1) make a difference and (2) shape department's direction. As part of the 2010 study, the following two additional questions were added: (1) What are the challenges in serving as a chair? and (2) Should collegiality be the fourth criteria for tenure decisions? Overall, in the four years of our research, 1,972 surveys were mailed out and 831 surveys were returned for a 42.1 percent return rate. What follows are analyses from the 2008, 2009, and 2010 studies and an analysis of the combined data from the four years of the study.

Results of the 2008 Survey

The message is clear from my many colleagues across the country: no end to the workload, no upper limit to the expectations, and no firm job description or educational training program to fall back on for support. Based on the assumption that no one else wanted to serve as chair, formulated over the data obtained during this study, the research in 2008 yielded the following results regarding the question, "Why do you remain as department chair?" (respondents could choose more than one answer):

1. No one else in the department will do it	43.3%
2. More money	38.7%
3. Stepping-stone in career	32.7%
4. Reduced teaching load	24.0%
5. Ability to hire faculty	22.7%
6. Control of budget	18.7%
7. Prestige	17.3%

8. Summer pay	13.3%
9. Released time	11.3%

Modification of the Survey Instrument—2009

Based on formal focus groups and informal discussions with chairs, the survey instrument was modified in 2009. The results were significant, both mathematically and philosophically, and show in the following the reason(s) why chairs remain in this position (again, respondents could choose more than one response):

1. Make a difference	85.8%
2. Shape department's direction	83.1%
3. Career advancement	39.1%
4. No one else in the department will do it	35.9%
5. More money	31.1%
6. Ability to hire faculty	24.7%
7. Reduced teaching load	17.4%
8. Control of budget	12.6%
9. Prestige	12.1%
10. Summer pay	11.5%

Collegiality and Challenges—2010 Survey

In October 2010, we sent the same survey to 286 department chairs and 104 surveys were returned for a 36.4 percent return rate. This survey asked two additional questions. The first question was, "Should collegiality be the fourth criterion for tenure decisions?" The respondents could answer either yes, no, or not sure to this question. The second question was, "Please indicate the challenges you face in serving as department chair." The respondents could select from a list of sixteen challenges and were asked to answer yes or no to each question. The following represents how the people answered each of the two questions:

1. Should collegiality be the fourth criterion for tenure decisions?
   - Seventy-six people (73.1%) answered yes.
   - Twelve people (11.5%) answered no.
   - Sixteen people (15.4%) answered not sure.
2. Challenges in serving as department chair. The percentage indicates those people who signified that, yes, this is a challenge to their chairpersonship:
   - Dealing with bureaucracy   65.4%
   - Lack of time to devote to individual research   61.5%
   - Stress associated with the job   60.6%
   - Dealing with noncollegial, uncivil faculty   58.7%
   - Excessive workload   57.7%

Demographics of Department Chairs

Of note, the satisfaction of the department chairs remained steadfast throughout the four years of the survey; consistently over 85 percent were either satisfied or very satisfied. Interestingly, the other variable that was equally constant was the lack of formal department chair education or training; each year of the study more than 96 percent of the respondents indicated that they had no formal training or education. Although several individuals surveyed did have some management training, the majority (more than 80 percent) did not, leaving them unprepared for myriad tasks that lay before them. Russ Olwell (2009) wrote that "most faculty, who have no academic leadership training, need real support to make this career transition a successful one. Drawn from the ranks of faculty, many new department chairs have virtually no training or resources to draw on in their new expanded role, and often feel isolated" (p. 7). Of interest is that this four-year study reveals a department chair satisfaction level synonymous with optimism and hope, not isolation or despair. Following is an analysis of the data obtained from 831 department chairs throughout the four years of this study.

Pleasant and Unpleasant Tasks

The results of the surveys revealed that there are many pleasant duties that chairs perform, and the most important ones revolve around the individuals they interact with. Following is a list of the pleasant tasks that chairs reported, along with the percentage of respondents who reported each task as pleasant.

Pleasant Tasks

1. Interpersonal communication tasks	89.8%
2. Encouraging professional development of department faculty	86.5%
3. Representing the department at professional meetings	82.2%
4. Interacting with administration on behalf of department	79.3%
5. Developing and initiating long-range department programs, plans, and goals	79.3%
6. Recruiting new full-time faculty	77.1%
7. Encouraging faculty research and publications	75.6%
8. Planning and reviewing curriculum, academic programs, and courses	73.9%
9. Retaining untenured faculty	73.6%
10. Department organizational tasks	72.1%

The results of the surveys also indicated those unpleasant tasks that chairs are required to perform.

Unpleasant Tasks

1. Terminating part-time adjunct faculty	78.7%
2. Terminating nonteaching personnel	73.0%
3. Terminating full-time faculty	71.2%
4. Maintaining morale and reducing conflicts among faculty	57.2%
5. Requesting additional resources from administration	56.1%
6. Evaluating full-time faculty members	53.3%

Clearly, there are many positive duties that chairs perform, and the most important ones revolve around the individuals with whom they interact. Whether they are *encouraging* or *retaining*, the themes of the pleasant tasks are two-pronged: building the department and building relationships. Conversely, the top three unpleasant tasks all use the word *terminating*, which would equate to "tearing down" relationships. When people describe their employment satisfaction, they often say, "It's not the job, it's the people." With department chairs, "the job" is all about "the people," and because the department's success is dependent on those people, chairs truly believe that the sum is greater than the parts.

Skills and Competencies

A literature review indicated that there are sixteen competencies that department chairs should possess, which we asked respondents to rate first as necessary (yes or no) and then rate as either essential, desired, or not needed. As a true indication of the diverse skill set needed to function effectively as a department chair, fourteen of the sixteen competencies were rated as necessary by 87 percent or more of the respondents. Following are the results listed by the respondents as being "essential," along with the percentage of responses for each of the top seven competencies.

Essential Competencies

1. Ability to communicate effectively	86.4%
2. Character and integrity	81.6%
3. Decision-making ability	81.0%
4. Trustworthiness	80.6%
5. Leadership skills	79.1%
6. Problem-solving ability	78.0%
7. Interpersonal skills	76.8%

Ranking of Importance of Competencies

In an effort to further refine the skills deemed necessary by the respondents, we asked them to rank in order of importance the seven most crucial competencies needed to be an effective department chair. The scores were weighted according to the responses received: a rank of 1 was awarded 5 points, a rank of 2 was awarded 4 points, and so on. The nine highest ranked skills and competencies, as reported by the respondents, were as follows:

1. Ability to communicate effectively

2. Character and integrity

3. Leadership skills

4. Interpersonal skills

5. Decision-making ability

6. Problem-solving ability

7. Organizational ability

8. Trustworthiness

9. Program or course innovation and development

The theme, as also reported in those pleasant and unpleasant duties that chairs perform, revolves around department relationships. It is important to note that many of the skills listed (such as leadership and problem solving) are not simply innate but could be taught in some type of instructional setting such as a chair's institute, where new chairs could be paired with internal mentors.

Throughout this research, I have always been puzzled as to why people want to become or remain a department chair. This bewilderment may seem odd in view of the fact that I have served as a department chair for more than twenty-eight of my thirty-six years in higher education. It was very illuminating to see that chairs describe their satisfaction with the job as being directly related to the relationships they have with the people they work with. I have spoken with many former chairs who retired from the academy. The great majority of them, when asked what they missed the most about no longer working, responded that they missed the daily interactions with their colleagues. However, when they were left to deal with a nasty, uncivil, and toxic faculty member in their department the satisfaction level was understandably diminished. It was directly through my personal discussions with current and former department chairs that something insightful came to light: this job was more than merely "money," more than just "career aspirations," and more than just "a burden that no one else would shoulder."

References

Chapter One: Collegiality and Civility in Higher Education

Buller, J. *The Essential Department Chair*. San Francisco: Jossey-Bass, 2006.

Chu, D. *The Department Chair Primer: Leading and Managing Academic Departments*. Bolton, MA: Anker Publishing, 2006.

Cipriano, R. E. "Thorns Where There Once Was a Rose Garden." *Academic Leader*, 2009a, *25*(5), 8–9.

Cipriano, R. E. "Uncivil Faculty: The Chairs' Role." *The Department Chair*, 2009b, *20*(1), 15, 17–18.

Cipriano, R. E., and Riccardi, R. L. "Self-Perceived Expectations of Chairs." *The Department Chair*, 2008, *18*(4), 3–5.

Cipriano, R. E., and Riccardi, R. L. "The Chair Conundrum: Individually Professed Prospects of Department Chairs." *The Department Chair*, 2010a, *20*(3), 15–18.

Cipriano, R. E., and Riccardi, R. L. "A Three-Year Study of Chairs: Changing the World, One Department at a Time." *The Department Chair*, 2010b, *21*(1), 23–26.

Cipriano, R. E., and Riccardi, R. L. "What Is Unique About Chairs: A Continuing Exploration." *The Department Chair*, 2010c, *20*(4), 26–28.

Collaborative on Academic Careers in Higher Education (COACHE). (2007). *COACHE Highlights Report, 2007*. Cambridge, MA: Author.

Coffman, J. R. *Work and Peace in Academe*. Bolton, MA: Anker Publishing, 2005.

della Cava, M. "What Happened to Civility?" *USA Today*, September 15, 2009, p. 1.

Fogg, P. "Academic Therapists: Hoping to Avoid Lawsuits and Rancor, More Colleges Use Conflict-Resolution Experts." *Chronicle of Higher Education*, March 21, 2003, pp. A12–A13.

Gappa, J. M., Austin, A. E., and Trice, A. G. *Rethinking Faculty Work: Higher Education's Strategic Imperative.* San Francisco: Jossey-Bass, 2007.

Hecht, I.W.D., Higgerson, M. L., Gmelch, W. H., and Tucker, A. *The Department Chair as Academic Leader.* Phoenix: The Oryx Press, 1999.

Kezar, A. "Pluralistic Leadership: Incorporating Diverse Voices." *Journal of Higher Education,* 2000, *71*(6), 722–743.

Lucas, A. F., and Associates. *Leading Academic Change: Essential Roles for Department Chairs.* San Francisco: Jossey-Bass, 2000.

Olwell, R. "Why New Department Chairs Need Coaching." *Academic Leader,* 2009, *23*(6), 7.

Pew Higher Education Roundtable. "Double Agent." *Policy Perspectives,* 1996, *63*(3), 1–12.

Rand, A. *Anthem.* New York: Penguin Putnam, 1995, p. 49.

Twale, D. J, and De Luca, B. M. *Faculty Incivility.* San Francisco: Jossey-Bass, 2008.

Chapter Two: Respectful Codes and Hiring for Collegiality

Buller, J. *The Essential Department Chair.* San Francisco: Jossey-Bass, 2006.

Falcone, P. *96 Great Interview Questions to Ask Before You Hire.* New York: AMACOM, 2008.

Chapter Three: Strategies for Promoting Collegiality

Buller, J. *The Essential Department Chair.* San Francisco: Jossey-Bass, 2006.

Cipriano, R. E., and Riccardi, R. L. "A Three-Year Study of Chairs: Changing the World, One Department at a Time." *The Department Chair,* 2010, *21*(1), 23–26.

Chu, D. *The Department Chair Primer.* Bolton, MA: Anker Publishing, 2006.

Coffman, J. R. *Work and Peace in Academe.* Bolton, MA: Anker Publishing, 2005.

Freiberg, K., and Freiberg, J. *Nuts.* New York: Broadway Books, 1996.

Higgerson, M. L. *Communication Skills for Department Chairs.* Bolton, MA: Anker Publishing, 1996.

James, H. *The Principles of Psychology.* Vol. 2. New York: Henry Holt, p. 392.

McCullough, D. *Truman.* New York: Simon & Schuster, 1992, p. 564.

Chapter Four: Managing Conflict Within the Department

Berra, L. P. "Tune into Body Language." *Dealing with Difficult People*. Overland Park, KS: Park University Enterprises, 2003, p. 5.

Cheldelin, S. I., and Lucas, A. F. *Academic Administrator's Guide to Conflict Resolution*. San Francisco: Jossey-Bass, 2004.

Cipriano, R. E., and Riccardi, R. L. "A Three-Year Study of Chairs: Changing the World, One Department at a Time." *The Department Chair*, 2010, *21*(1), 23–26.

Creamer, E. "Collaborators' Attitudes About Differences of Opinion." *Journal of Higher Education*, 2004, *75*, 556.

Higgerson, M. L. *Communication Skills for Department Chairs*. Bolton, MA: Anker Publishing, 1996.

Pickering, P. "How to Handle Conflict and Confrontation." *National Press Publications*. Shawnee Mission, KS: Rockhurst University Continuing Education Center, 2000.

Sutton, R. I. *The No Asshole Rule: Building A Civilized Workforce and Surviving One That Isn't*. New York: Warner Business Books, 2007.

Chapter Five: University-Wide Responsibilities in Promoting a Collegial Campus

Buller, J. "The Perception Problem," *Academic Leader*, April 2010, *26*(4), 24.

Callan, P. "College May Become Unaffordable for Most in U.S." *The New York Times*, December 3, 2008, p. A19.

Gappa, J. M., Austin, A. E., and Trice, A. G. *Rethinking Faculty Work*. San Francisco: Jossey-Bass, 2007.

Goldin, C. "Tales Out of School," *The New York Times*, February 7, 2010, p. A26.

Greenblatt, A. "Higher Purpose: America Produces the World's Best Universities, but Not Enough Graduates. Can States Fix Higher Education?" *Governing*, September 13, 2007. [www.governing.com/topics/education/Higher-Purpose.html].

Chapter Six: Structural Realignment, Budgetary Support, and Cyberbullying

AAC&U National Panel. *Greater Expectations: A New Vision for Learning as a Nation Goes to College*. Washington, DC: Association of American Colleges and Universities, 2002.

Barker, C. M. *Liberal Arts Education for a Global Society*. New York: Carnegie Corporation, 2000.

Beatty, E., and Page, R. A., Jr. "Leadership as Place." In Jon Wergin (ed.), *Leadership in Place*. Bolton, MA: Anker Publishing, 2007, pp. 192–223.

Cipriano, R. E. "Uncivil Faculty: The Chairs' Role." *The Department Chair*, 2009, *20*(1), *15*, 17–18.

"Collaborative Partnerships Between University and Academic Affairs: A Model." Presentation at the 19th Annual Conference on the First-Year Experience, University of South Carolina, Columbia, February 18–22, 2001. (Refereed).

Fogg, P. "Academic Therapists: Hoping to Avoid Lawsuits and Rancor, More Colleges Use Conflict-Resolution Experts." *Chronicle of Higher Education*, March 21, 2003, pp. A12–A13.

Guskin, A. E., and Marcy, M. B. "Dealing with the Future Now: Principles for Creating a Vital Company in a Climate of Restricted Resources." *Change*, 2003, *35*(4), 10–21.

Rand, A. *The Romantic Manifesto: A Philosophy of Literature*. Rev. ed. New York: Signet, 1975, p. 131.

Rosovsky, H. *The University: An Owner's Manual*. New York: W. W. Norton, 1990.

Wergin, J. F. *Departments That Work: Building and Sustaining Cultures of Excellence in Academic Programs*. Bolton, MA: Anker Publishing, 2003.

Chapter Seven: Case Law Regarding Collegiality in Higher Education

American Association of University Professors. "On Collegiality as a Criterion for Faculty Evaluation." *Policy Documents and Reports*. (*9th ed.*) Washington, DC: Author, 1999 [www.aaup.org/AAUP/pubsres/policydocs/contents/collegiality.htm].

Auburn University. "Faculty Personnel Policies and Procedures: Tenure Criteria and Considerations: Collegiality," February 11, 2011. [www.auburn.edu/academic/provost/handbook/policies.html].

Buller, J. L. *The Essential Department Chair*. Bolton, MA: Anker Publishing, 2006.

Buller, J. L. "The Perception Problem." *Academic Leader*, 2010, *26*(4), 2–3.

Connell, M. A., and Savage, F. G. "Does Collegiality Count?" *Academe*, 2001, *87*(6), 37–41.

CSU-AAU&P and Board of Trustees. *Collective Bargaining Agreement*. Hartford: Connecticut State University System, 2007–2011, p. 12.

Owens, R. G. *Organizational Behavior in Education*. (8th ed.) New York: Pearson, 2004.

Sutton, R. I. *The No Asshole Rule: Building A Civilized Workforce and Surviving One That Isn't*. New York: Warner Business Books, 2007, p. 27.

Trower, C. Collaborative on Academic Careers in Higher Education (COACHE). *Chronicle of Higher Education*, November 4, 2008.

Appendix: A Four-Year Study of Department Chairs

Cipriano, R. E., and Riccardi, R. L. "Self-Perceived Expectations of Chairs." *The Department Chair*, 2008, *18*(4), 3–5.

Cipriano, R. E., and Riccardi, R. L. "The Chair Conundrum: Individually Professed Prospects of Department Chairs." *The Department Chair*, 2010a, *20*(3), 15–18.

Cipriano, R. E., and Riccardi, R. L. "What Is Unique About Chairs: A Continuing Exploration." *The Department Chair*, 2010b, *20*(4), 26–28.

Olwell, R. "Why New Department Chairs Need Coaching." *Academic Leader*, 2009, *23*(6), 7.

Acknowledgments

This book is the result of the efforts of many people who believe in the values of collegiality. First and foremost I would like to thank Jeff Buller for writing the Foreword to the book. Jeff is a tireless worker who continues to amaze people with the quality and the amount of work he produces. In addition, and equally as important, his sense of humor can brighten a room. I have enjoyed our humorous e-mails and telephone conversations. I would also like to personally thank Ellen Beatty for taking time from her busy schedule to contribute Chapter Six to the book. Ellen has been my dear friend and colleague for more than thirty years. I was privileged to serve as chair in the school when Ellen was dean. I realized what a great leader she was, and she continued to contribute greatly to the university when she moved into the role of vice president for academic affairs.

Many colleagues across the United States gave of their time to thoughtfully respond to the collegiality questions I posed to them. You will read the quotes of the following people who contributed greatly to the balance that this book attempts: Jerry Chmielewski, Roger Coles, Walter Gmelch, Susan Hannam, Tim Hatfield, Doug Lees, Jim MacGregor, Sue Ouellette, Bruce Russell, Stuart Schleien, Bill Swift, and Bill Williams. I thank them for their swift and attentive responses. I would also like to thank Sheryl Fullerton of Jossey-Bass who kept me on task and motivated. She always provided useful comments. The driving force behind this book, as she has been throughout my life and our forty-four years of marriage, is my wife, Raffaela. Her kindness and generous spirit qualifies her as the true expert on collegiality and civility in our family.

The Author

Robert Cipriano received his doctorate in therapeutic recreation with a cognate area of study in higher education from New York University. He has contributed chapters to three textbooks and has published two other books and more than 130 journal articles and manuscripts. Bob has served as a department chair for twenty-eight of his thirty-six years in higher education. He has been given more than $9 million in foundation, state, and federal grants and contracts. Bob has served as an expert to review grants for the federal government on sixteen separate occasions. He has been invited to deliver more than two hundred presentations in the United States, Asia, and the Middle East and has provided consultant services to many colleges in the United States regarding collegiality and conflict management. He is currently Professor Emeritus in the Department of Recreation and Leisure Studies at Southern Connecticut State University.

Index